Living & Working in Portugal

Practical books that inspire

Getting a Job Abroad
The handbook for the international jobseeker

Retire Abroad
Your guide to a full and happy retirement in a foreign country

Living and Working in Spain
The complete guide to a successful short or long-term stay

Teaching Abroad
How and where to find teaching and lecturing jobs worldwide

Buying a Property in Spain
An insider guide to finding a home in the sun

howtobooks

Please send for a free copy of the latest catalogue to:

How To Books
3 Newtec Place, Magdalen Road,
Oxford OX4 1RE, United Kingdom
info@howtobooks.co.uk
www.howtobooks.co.uk

Living & Working in
Portugal

*All you need to know
to enjoy life in Portugal*

3rd edition

SUE TYSON-WARD

howto books

For Mum, Dad, and Ed

Published by
How To Books Ltd, 3 Newtec Place,
Magdalen Road, Oxford OX4 1RE. United Kingdom.
Tel: (01865) 793806. Fax: (01865) 248780.
email: info@howtobooks.co.uk
http://www.howtobooks.co.uk

First publshed 1993
Second edition 2000
Third edition 2002

British Library Cataloguing in Publication Data.
A catalogue record for this book is available from
the British Library.

Cover design by Baseline Arts Ltd, Oxford
Produced for How To Books by Deer Park Productions
Typeset by PDQ Typesetting, Newcastle-under-Lyme, Staffs.
Printed and bound by Cromwell Press, Trowbridge, Wiltshire

NOTE: The material contained in this book is set out in good
faith for general guidance and no liability can be accepted for
loss or expense incurred as a result of relying in particular
circumstances on statements made in the book. Laws and
regulations are complex and liable to change, and readers should
check the current position with the relevant authorities before
making personal arrangements.

Contents

List of Illustrations

Preface
to the third edition

In the years since the writing of the first edition of this book, Portugal has undergone many changes, structurally, economically and in terms of its popularity for business and pleasure alike. Always a favourite choice of holiday-makers, it now attracts some 1½ million British visitors annually. Many of these enjoy its beautiful Algarve beaches and warm hospitality, some stay and forge a living for themselves and their families. Others are transferred to work in the larger towns on behalf of a growing number of multinational companies taking root in Portugal and benefiting from a clement economic climate.

Portugal has now enjoyed membership of the EU for over a decade, and is currently reaping the rewards of various financial subsidies that have led to large investment by companies such as VW, demonstrating the growing confidence in this country. The Portuguese people have forged ahead with training in areas such as computing, business and engineering, and are able to compete favourably with other nationalities – they are also multilingual, most of the younger people today being happy to communicate in French, English, German or Spanish as well as their mother tongue.

In 1998 the last great Exposition of this millennium (Expo 98) was held in Lisbon. A huge site on the side of the river

Tagus, hitherto an abandoned oil refinery, was transformed into an awe-inspiring exhibition and entertainment area, and played host to more people than actually live in Portugal itself! As a direct result of all the structural work undertaken leading up to Expo, Lisbon now boasts an extended (and extending) underground system, a new bridge over the river (the Ponte Vasco da Gama), and Europe's largest oceanarium – a legacy on the Expo site. Elsewhere in the country new motorway infrastructure is easing communication between north and south, and high-speed modern trains now link Lisbon with Oporto, the south and Spain.

At the same time Portugal maintains its links with agriculture, and the land is an important factor in many people's lives. And that remains part of the appeal Portugal will continue to have for the many people who visit it: the slower pace of life and the friendliness of people in rural areas are things we all long for at the start of this highly technological new millennium.

Portugal offers something for everyone, and I hope this new edition of *Living and Working in Portugal* will continue to guide those who wish to try life out there for more than a brief two-week holiday. In the words of Jorge Sampaio (the President of Portugal), at the opening of Expo:

> '*O país que vos recebe é um país de liberdade, aberto à modernidade . . . e um povo hospitaleiro e aberto ao convívio com os outros . . .*'

'The country which receives you is a country of freedom, open to modern ideas... and a welcoming people keen to get on and socialise with others...'

Enjoy it!

Sue Tyson-Ward

Acknowledgements

Over the years many people have kindly sent me information and documentation on aspects of life in Portugal. I would particularly like to thank the following for their assistance in this new edition:

João Lança Cardeira (Automóvel Club de Portugal), Nigel Thomas (The British Council in Lisbon), The British Embassy in Lisbon, The Portuguese National Tourist Office, Direcção Geral de Turismo in Lisbon, Departamento de Estrangeiros in Lisbon, Mr Ronnie Price (Portuguese-UK Chamber of Commerce), European Council of International Schools, Maria Amélia Estrela, The Council of Europe, International Women in Portugal, Porto Mothers' Group, Mr F. X. T. Fernandes, Ann and Harold Greenhalgh, Mr A Dixon, The UK Benefits Agency and Mr Ken McKenzie.

Fig. 1. Map of Portugal.

Introducing Portugal

OVERVIEW: THE GEOGRAPHY OF PORTUGAL

Where, then, to visit whilst you are here? Portugal is an extremely beautiful and varied country to visit. Chapter 12 contains some suggestions for days out, but here is an overview of the different regions and their attractions. Further Reading lists travel guides which you may find useful as an additional source of information.

Provinces

Minho	the most northern area
Douro	river 'of Gold'
Trás-os-Montes	beyond the hills
Beira Alta	upper Beira
Beira Baixa	lower Beira
Beira Litoral	coastal Beira
Ribatejo	along banks of the Tejo (River Tagus)
Estremadura	extreme part of Roman Empire
Alto Alentejo	upper Alentejo (Além Tejo = away from Tejo)
Baixo Alentejo	lower Alentejo
Algarve	Al Gharb (= Moorish, The West)

It is also now common to refer to Portugal in terms of the following regions:

Norte – North
Centro – Centre
Lisboa e Vale de Tejo – Lisbon and Tagus Valley
Alentejo
Algarve

A useful set of information sheets numbered 1-8, called *Portugal Travelfacts*, including the islands of Madeira and the Azores, are available on request from the Portuguese National Tourist Office (address at back of book) as well as a full range of regional brochures.

The landscape of the country alters dramatically as you journey from North to South. The wine-growing areas of the Minho and Douro valleys are lush, green fertile lands with the typical terraced slopes of the vineyards. Nearby, the National Park Peneda Gerês is a wonderful expanse of protected countryside, as is the colourful tropical Buçaco forest. The whole northern region as far down as Lisbon is full of fine historical buildings, sites of prehistoric remains and beautiful palaces and gardens. The coastline stretches down from the Spanish border (Galicia) to the Lisbon peninsular in miles of silver unspoilt beaches. Inland, the hilly areas of rugged scenery and tranquil settings are a haven away from life itself. Many areas are very basic in terms of lifestyle and architecture (granite dominates, some villages actually growing up out of the very rock), but very rich in tradition, folklore and cuisine. The area is also the home of the Serra da Estrela – a nature reserve and winter sports centre at the highest point in the country. Hunting wild boar is popular here as is the attraction of a variety of thermal baths.

South onto the great plains the scenery changes once more – the pastures around the upper stretches of the River Tagus are the traditional breeding ground of the Ribatejan bulls. Here, the home of bull and horse, the whole feel of the region is colour, movement and spirit. As the endless plains of the Alentejo take over, colour becomes a blend of hues, and agriculture on the once large estates (many of them now cooperatives) is predominantly that of cork and olive production. Finally there is the Moorish-influenced Algarve, where vestiges of Arab lifestyles still abound in architecture, names, and cuisine. Portugal has something to offer everyone whatever form of landscape you enjoy.

THE PORTUGUESE PEOPLE...OS PORTUGUESES

Most visitors to Portugal tend to agree that the Portuguese are 'so welcoming', 'very friendly', 'eager to please', and 'easy going', albeit 'sometimes lacking in service skills'.

However, it is misleading to adhere strictly to generalities, especially where national characteristics are concerned. In fact, if you were to travel from North to South, you would quickly notice how attitudes, behaviour and beliefs vary from region to region. From the Northern areas isolated in geography and time, where the rural dwellers, who have always strongly depended on the village priest for guidance, may distrust the arrival of any stranger to their parts, to the cosmopolitan and busy lifestyles of Oporto and Lisbon, and finally down to the ex-pat enclaves of the Algarve, where many Portuguese have learnt that rich pickings are to be made in the tourism industry –

characteristics change.

But on the whole the Portuguese are very friendly, especially if you make the effort to try and speak at least some of their language. Then you will see a broad smile take over their face as they exclaim 'fala português' (you speak Portuguese!) Their rather slow (usually very frustrating) service in shops, banks and post offices is in part due to the many years of dictatorial rule under Salazar, when a strict regime controlled all parts of a person's life. It can be quite frustrating waiting to be served when assistants ignore you to carry on their chat. Service skills are yet to be instilled in a mostly undertrained workforce. And don't be surprised to have to fill in official documents in at least triplicate.

Much has been written about the famous Portuguese emotion of *saudade*, or great nostalgia for times, people and places far-off, and many an attempt has been made to define the Portuguese character in relation to this yearning for their glorious past. In fact Portugal's entry into the EU in 1986 was seen by some as proof that she was once more looking outwards from her own land and seeking fortune abroad as she had done back in the 15th and 16th centuries. Most Portuguese today, although naturally proud of their great past, don't dwell on it, and concern themselves more with everyday problems.

RELIGION, BEHAVIOUR, LIFESTYLES

Religion

One traditional feature which is as strong as ever is the role of the Catholic Church in many Portuguese lives. Northern Portugal has always been considered the stronghold of the Church, whereas the Alentejo and the Algarve have mostly been more liberal and religion has not featured so fervently in lifestyles. Each town though, whether North or South, has its own religious processions and festivals throughout the religious calendar. The great month is June, with celebrations for the Saints Anthony, John and Peter (**os Santos Populares**) especially in Oporto and Lisbon; then the whole month is dedicated to feasting (grilled chicken and sardines, salad and crusty bread) and dancing, with each borough (**bairro**) setting up its own carnival-style venue.

One of the interesting facts about religion in Portugal is that strong Catholic beliefs live side by side with some unusual, almost pagan attitudes, mostly in the North. Although frowned upon by the Catholic Church, they are nevertheless tolerated. For example, festivals such as 'Midnight Baptism' for unborn children, and the 'procession of the dead', where the ghost of the next parishioner to die is seen, are common in the North. If you visit some churches, you may see a whole array of waxen limbs hanging up. These, along with tresses of hair, photos and jewellery, are all token offerings to saints who have 'helped' someone in some way, such as to recover from illness. If you have the opportunity to visit the famous shrine of Fátima, north of Lisbon, you will see examples of people on pilgrimages (**romarias**) who have walked for miles on their knees, again as a sign of fulfilment of a 'promise', this time to the Virgin Mary. There are innumerable religious festivals in each region throughout the year. The following dates are the official national holidays:

National holidays

1 Jan	New Year's Day	10 June	Camões Day (Portugal Day)
Feb/March	Shrove Tuesday (Carnival)	15 Aug	Our Lady of Assumption
Mar/April	Good Friday/Easter	5 Oct	Republic Day
25 April	Liberation Day	1 Nov	All Saints
1 May	Labour Day	1 Dec	Independence Day
June	Corpus Christi	8 Dec	Immaculate Conception
		25 Dec	Christmas

In addition, Lisbon celebrates St Anthony's Day on 13 June, and in Porto St John is celebrated on 24 June.

Tourist offices in each town will always provide details of local celebrations. If you visit any religious festival, or enter a church, please dress properly. You will always see the Portuguese family very well-dressed, not only for church, but also for evening and Sunday strolls around the town.

Behaviour

A vital component of Portuguese behaviour is that of good manners and polite address. There is great respect for young children and for the old, with family ties still much stronger than in the UK. Forms of address can be rather confusing, as there are a variety of ways to call someone 'You'. The most common, polite versions are O SENHOR (for men)/A SENHORA (for ladies), but it is not uncommon to hear even more outdated forms such as 'A SUA EXCELÊNCIA' in references to political leaders and heads of state. It is usual for ladies of a certain age or standing to be called SENHORA DONA + their Christian name; sometimes dropping SENHORA is allowed.

In smaller, rural villages, inhabitants tend to have a conservative, traditional outlook on life, where all that is 'out of the ordinary' may be seen as a threat to the village and family nucleus, whereas in cities such as Oporto and

Lisbon every facet of life can be experienced in all its glory. Attitudes to women have changed since the revolution. Before, it was commonplace for a husband to treat his spouse exactly as if he owned her – opening her mail and monitoring her movements. After 1974 new laws were introduced giving women more rights, but as in all Latin countries many women still find the macho character prevails. However, you do now find women filtering through into once male-dominated professions, albeit very slowly. In the countryside, particularly, the social make-up is noticeably matriarchal, with the mother the pivot of the household. These are gutsy women, to be admired, respected and sometimes feared.

Lifestyles

Lifestyles vary greatly, though a common trait is the casual approach to life and its problems. What many tourists mistakenly call the 'mañana' approach (which is Spanish), has an element of truth in it, but it's not so much that things are left until tomorrow as an inherent inability to think ahead, the lack of logical thought in many cases which can leave many a northern European fraught with frustration in a business or even social context.

Northern Portuguese, around Oporto and the wine districts, are considered the industrialists of the country, busy people with comfortable lifestyles. If you look at the folklore dress of the different regions, you will notice that the further north the group, the more gold chains the women are adorned with – representation of their relative wealth. On the other hand, the northern territories bordering on Spain are the complete opposite. Here, in regions like Trás-os-Montes (Beyond-the-Hills) life has been compared with the rest of Europe in the middle ages. Time has stood still here and some villages have only recently received electricity; most use a river as a water supply and life is generally hard-going. Agricultural methods are outdated – some still use oxen and hand ploughs – but enough food is produced to feed everyone; beggars are not seen on the streets and everyone rallies round to help each other.

In contrast, the cosmopolitan capital of Lisbon boasts a mixture of the new and the old, not only in its architecture for example, but in its pace – the bustle of a busy working city, coupled with tourism, and on the outskirts (where most visitors might not venture) the slums and shanty towns. However, it must be said that apart from these unfortunate locations and the odd beggar or two in large centres, poverty in this respect is not as outstandingly noticeable as even in the UK now. Apart from gypsy children in the Algarve who are sent into towns to beg, whilst the menfolk wait on the outskirts in their carts, it is rare to find a town inundated with alcoholics, people in shop doorways or yobbish youths kicking rubbish around and being offensive.

The Algarve of course has found a prosperity all of its own, with tourism, but this has brought its own problems in terms of crime. Gangs have found rich pickings in villas where foreign-registered cars are parked outside, but crime also originates from the ex-pats themselves – reports once showed that the big timeshare complexes were being jealously guarded by each company, which had even brought in hired hitmen to warn off touters on their territory. On the whole, though, crime in Portugal is less than in other European countries. Much of that reported involves family disputes, rival factions, petty theft, and some crimes of passion. Unfortunately, drugs are starting to make an impact, particularly in certain parts of the capital, but murder of children, rape, bank robberies, are rare and would shock this generally peaceful people. As long as you are sensible, the streets in Portugal are safe to go out on.

POLITICS

Portugal is a parliamentary democracy with a stable and settled government. The President of the Republic (at the time of writing Jorge Sampaio, of the Socialist party) is officially the Head of State and Commander-in-Chief of the Armed Forces. The President is democratically elected by the people. He, in turn, appoints the Prime Minister and the Council of Ministers nominated by him. The President represents the nation as a whole, whilst the day-to-day running of the country rests with the Government. The Parliament (**Assembleia da República**) currently has 230 members elected by the people.

The country is divided into areas for administrative purposes, with 18 official districts and two autonomous regions. These are further sub-divided into municipalities and then parishes. Each district has its own local government, with District Governors (**Governadores**) appointed by the Minister for Internal Administration. The municipalities are administered through a local council (**Câmara**

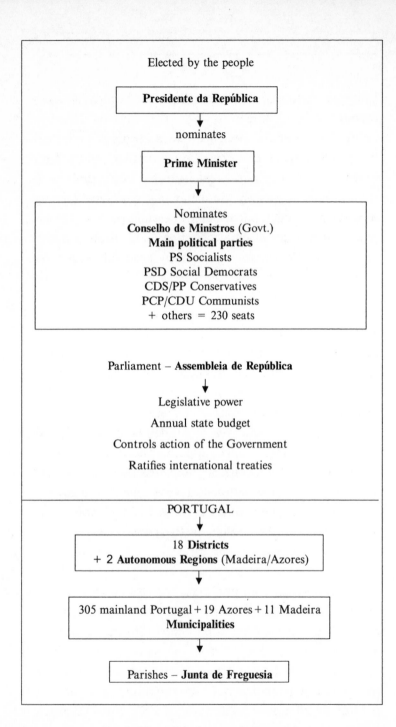

Fig. 2. The political system in Portugal.

Muncipal), each led by a **Presidente** elected by the local residents.

Portugal is a key player in various international organisations, including the EU, United Nations, NATO (a founding member), PALOPS (Association of Portuguese-speaking countries in Africa), CPLP (Commonwealth of Portuguese-speaking countries, launched in 1996), and adheres to the GATT (General Agreement of Trade and Tariffs).

THE ECONOMY

Recent years have seen a surge in confidence within the Portuguese business world. Indeed, its recent growth rate has been the highest in Europe. The Socialist government is backing investment and working closely with industry, adding to a positive outlook. Prime Minister António Guterres has lead a country outperforming all economic expectations, and bringing Portugal firmly into the next era of the country's development. He has been determined to push ahead with modernisation, which since joining the EU in 1986, has heralded a new era in living standards, and with unemployment at around 4.4%, and sustained growth in foreign investment he has had much to feel content about, although current indications point to a slowing down of this success rate.

Portugal's chief exports have always been textiles and footwear, cork (the world's leading producer), wine, ceramics and canned fish, but now huge foreign investment means that industrial parks are developing, encompassing a range of business projects. The most talked about in recent years was the agreement between Ford and VW to build a car plant in Setúbal (25 miles south of Lisbon), the biggest foreign investment ever made in the country. Further, recent developments include investments by Siemens and interest from the USA.

Of course tourism accounts for a huge chunk of the economy, with ever-increasing numbers of visitors (mainly Spanish, followed by Brits and Germans), almost 50% of whom stay in the Algarve. The number of British visitors has increased steadily over the past decade, with well over one and a half million visiting Portuguese shores each year. Portugal is, however, becoming more concerned about promoting quality of tourism, not quantity. Investment is being made, not in providing more hotels, but by improving existing facilities, creating more golf courses, conference centres and cultural ideas. A weaning off the Algarve as a holiday spot, towards central and Northern areas, where 'quality' visitors may enjoy a different type of holiday, is also envisaged. The Deputy Mayor for Culture in Cascais-Estoril recently said: 'This is a town for tourism and leisure visited by wealthy people, but we also want to present a cultural dimension by exploiting an exciting history that saw the greatest intellectuals of this century pass through here, by offering people who come here something more than casinos, sun, beaches and a motor-racing course: the spiritual enrichment only culture can provide.' However, the 3,000 hours of sunshine annually will continue to make the Algarve a top attraction.

THE LEGAL SYSTEM

Every citizen has the right to access the judicial system, as laid down by the Constitution. Lack of financial means is not a bar to legal redress. The courts are autonomous and are bound only to the established law of the land and the demands of the Constitution. Generally speaking, they adhere to the traditional principles of an independent legal system, but the lack of cohesive, organised bureaucracy within the system itself has led to a large backlog of cases, with some people waiting years for their cases to come to court, and a great lack of 'Legal Aid', especially in the case of foreign defendants. The court system can be illustrated as shown in Figure 3.

Supreme Court The High Court – sits in Lisbon, can judge on civil, criminal, commercial cases.

Courts of Secondary Jurisdiction Act as Courts of Appeal. Cases over a certain limit can appeal to the Supreme Court.

Courts of Primary Jurisdiction		
County Courts General cases, criminal, family, minors, labour cases. Court's decision final in cases under a certain value. Over this threshold you can appeal to the Courts of Secondary Jurisdiction.	**Admin Courts** Local and national government matters.	**Tax Courts** Tax cases.

Fig. 3. The legal system in Portugal.

There is also a Constitutional Court, dealing with matters related to the Constitution. The main crimes in Portugal include presentation of bad cheques, minor assault, and disobedience. The figures for murder, manslaughter and traffic homicide are minimal.

HISTORY

You can't go very far without noticing reminders of the past – in street names, for example:

25 de Abril – date of the 1974 revolution
5 de Outubro – beginning of the Republic in 1910
Praça de Camões – Portugal's national poet
Praça dos Restauradores – the restorers of independence after Spanish rule

Similar reminders are found in monuments – the Torre de Belém and monument to the era of the discoveries in Lisbon, the great Batalha monastery built in 1385 to commemorate victory over the Spanish, the school of navigation in Sagres, and the red Moorish castle in Silves, in the Algarve – not to mention the many elegant buildings which have been home to royalty and clergy throughout Portugal's history.

Looking back through Portuguese history one can see that life has not been easy for this small country of only 10 million inhabitants, and yet they have much to be proud of. It was colonised by the Romans, overrun by northern warriors such as the Goths and Visigoths, and then dominated for so long, as were the Spanish, by the Moorish invasions, and you may be inclined to believe life became less hectic once the Moors had been driven out in the late 12th century – not so. Constant wranglings with the Spanish courts over supreme rule of the whole Iberian peninsula were to continue for centuries, with continual invasions by the Castilians. No wonder that the Portuguese take offence when spoken to in Spanish! A saying goes 'De Espanha nem bom vento nem bom casamento' (from Spain come neither fair winds nor good marriages). The Golden Era of the 15th and 16th centuries saw Portugal as world explorers (and exploiters) and at one point Spain and Portugal divided the known world between them. The 19th century also saw an expansionist period, when the Empire took over African colonies such as Angola, Mozambique, and Cape Verde. In more recent times history was dominated by the dictatorial regime of Salazar, with opinion polarised about the pros and cons of his rule.

The brief chronology on page 16 may serve as a guide to some of the important dates in Portuguese history.

CULTURAL LIFE

Portugal, as a country with a long history full of influences from external peoples, is home to magnificent architectural structures (from pre-history onwards), as well as superb art, furniture and literary collections mirroring and chronicling the events that shaped the country and its peoples. The Portuguese are swift to tell you where their museums and church buildings are, proud of their heritage. They will more often than not offer to escort you round such places and their enthusiasm can be difficult to refuse.

1143	Portugal recognised as a sovereign kingdom by Leon and Castile
1267	Castile gives up Algarve to Portugal and completes its modern territory
1373	Anglo-Portuguese Alliance (oldest in Europe and still in existence)
1419	First voyage of exploration (Madeira) on behalf of Prince Henry the Navigator – son of João I and Phillipa of Lancaster – daughter of John O'Gaunt, Duke of Lancaster
1498	Vasco da Gama reached India via the Cape of Good Hope
1500	Alvares Cabral reached Brazil
1510	Goa – seat of Portuguese vice-royalty of India
1518	*Canton*, first Portuguese ship to China
1518-45	East of India, New Guinea and Japan
1580-1640	Spanish rule – loss of some territories to the Dutch
1815	Brazil declared a kingdom
1822	Brazil became an independent empire
1877-87	African colonies established
1889	Brazil declared a republic
1910	Portugal declared a republic
1926	Military coup – state of dictatorship
1961	India occupies Goa/Angola guerilla war begins
1970	Salazar dies but regime continues
1974	25 April military coup. Revolution of the Carnations (Cravos) – bloodless
1986	Entry into EU
1998	Expo 98 – last big exposition of the millennium.

Fig. 4. Portugal's history at a glance.

There are many diverse cultural activities in which the Portuguese participate, indulging their appreciation of art, music, drama and dance. Many towns have a museum and a collection of fascinating monuments and buildings. Many places have at least a cinema (which is very cheap in Portugal), some venue to listen to music and locations to see arts and crafts. In the larger cities visits to the theatre, concerts or galleries of modern exhibitions are popular, and Portugal can boast not only international-scale venues in Lisbon and Oporto, but also many acclaimed artistes from various disciplines. The importance of the arts is finely illustrated by the fact that on the death of Amália Rodrigues, the Queen of *Fado* (Portugal's national music) in October 1999, three days of national mourning was declared! In 1998 José Saramago, one of Portugal's well-known writers, was awarded the Nobel prize for Literature. In 2001 Oporto was European City of Culture, contributing to a current renaissance in artistic creation.

In smaller towns and villages cultural activity may revolve around local folklore, with musical groups performing traditional dance and song. There are still some bull-rings in Portugal, although the passion for this is not as widespread as in neighbouring Spain. Sunny Sunday afternoons can often be enjoyed listening to bands in the town parks or squares. The Portuguese enjoy gatherings of family and friends, and often an evening out may centre around a good meal in a restaurant. When Portuguese people do go out it's never a rushed affair. Whole families, often with three or four generations, take their time enjoying the food and company, and often afterwards take a stroll around the square. Young children are often included in these evening sorties. Entertaining is usually out rather than at home, unlike some Northern European trends. Perhaps that is down to the clement weather (most of the time), or possibly the fact that the Portuguese love to be out and about greeting their friends and colleagues.

Culture in Portugal encompasses a whole range of activities. Suggestions and further ideas for specific entertainment and leisure can be found in Chapter 12 and the Regional Directory.

For a comprehensive exploration of the subject, try out my 'Teach Yourself Portuguese Language, Life and Culture' (details in reading list).

$$\left(2\right)$$

Getting There

PREPARING THE PAPERWORK

New EU (European Union) arrangements allow for free movement around EU member states for EU citizens, provided they have a National Identity card. In the UK recent discussions have brought the possibility of ID cards much closer, but until they are introduced you will need a current, valid passport to enter Portugal. Portugal has long been a stickler over documents for every aspect of life and it would still be prudent to double-check current requirements for your own visit with the Portuguese Embassy or Consulate nearest to you. Always carry with you photocopies (in triplicate if possible) of all documents, official letters, special licences. Depending on your reasons for visiting Portugal – education/business/retirement/pleasure, long or short-term – you may not need all of the following, but use this as a reference list, to be checked before you intend to make a move:

Possible documents required

+ Passport: although not required to be stamped, still needed as ID.

+ Valid visa: if you are a non-EU citizen, including Commonwealth citizens. Check with your nearest Portuguese Consulate.

- Work permit: see Chapter 5 on employment – may not be needed.

- Residence permit: does not have to be applied for in advance of arriving in Portugal. Once there, contact the local **Serviço de Estrangeiros** (Foreigners Dept) to apply for a permit – you will require proof of lodgings, social security number or health insurance and proof of financial means. NB: for temporary visits of up to 90 days no permit is needed, but all visitors have to fill in a declaration form within three days of arrival. Rules for non-EU nationals apply. Check at your nearest Portuguese Consulate.

- Car licence and other vehicle documents: see Chapter 9 on driving. UK/International or EU licence accepted for temporary visits. On expiry you will then need to apply for a Portuguese licence. Green card insurance required.

- Medical/insurance documents: **Form E111** is available from the Post Office for reciprocal health arrangements.

- Bank letters: see Chapter 8 on finance. Needed for opening certain types of bank accounts.

- Student ID, e.g. ISIC card: useful for obtaining travel discounts and range of reductions. If studying on a course, evidence of admission to it should be taken, plus confirmation of any scholarship or grant offered to you by the Portuguese Education Ministry.

- Birth and marriage certificates.

Others
Copies of CVs, letters of reference (professional and

character), letters of introduction, particularly if from a Portuguese of good standing in the community.

WHAT TO TAKE

How long you expect to stay, and your purpose there, will determine what sort of items you take with you. Household goods, furniture, electrical appliances can all be readily bought out there, as can all the bed linen, towels and tea cloths imaginable (many cotton items you would buy in the UK are made in Portugal). Of course you will always have your own personal effects, but apart from these the following check-list may give you some ideas:

- TVs – if you are taking your own it will have to be converted over to the Portuguese system (405 line; UK = 625 line). You will also require a completed application for a Portuguese TV licence, at the time of applying for your Baggage Certificate (see p. 31). It may be simpler just to buy in Portugal.

- All electrical appliances – you will require an adaptor from 3- to 2-pin plug. Once out there you can buy a stock of 2-pin plugs and change your appliances over. Be careful with these small plugs, as often they easily pull out of sockets.

- Electric fan – if you have one, a must in the hot weather, not only to cool you down, but also a good deterrent against the mosquitoes at night.

- Electric fire – few houses have adequate heating, if any at all, and the winter can be uncomfortably cold. However, these as with fans can be purchased quite reasonably.

- English language publications – reading matter, as books in English are few and expensive – another good reason for learning Portuguese!

- Your favourite provisions – one typical choice is a stock of teabags, as the Liptons variety available is a weak substitute. I know one lady who asks any visitors coming from the UK to bring her boxes of Yorkshire tea! Marmite and stock cubes are also useful extras.

- Photos of your family. The Portuguese love to see family pictures and this gives you a conversation starter.

CLOTHING

This subject always seems to pose a dilemma, especially when space in baggage is scant and uncertainties about length of stay are a factor. Ask yourselves the following questions:

- How long am I staying?
  — Short/long term

- What time of year is it on arrival?

- Will I still be there when the seasons change?

- Do I have any specific health requirements regarding body temperature?
  — Am I affected by heat/cold?

- Does my budget allow for buying clothes once there?

- How much space do I have?

Clothing is not always cheap unless you are prepared to enter into the fun of bartering at the monthly markets.

Even then, in tourist areas the vendors now know they can bump up their prices, and teeshirts, for example, can cost the same as you would pay in the UK. Usually jeans and men's trousers can be sniffed out a little cheaper, and, of course, if you can get out to some of the smaller towns away from the coast you should be able to find some bargains. Visits to some of the supermarket chains, such as Prisunic, can be worthwhile for cheaper clothing. Some areas also have cheap factory outlets, particularly around Oporto and the north.

Women's suits and dresses										
British	8	10	12	14	16	18	20	22		
European	36	38	40	42	44	46	48	50		
Women's shoes										
British	3	3½	4	4½	5	5½	6	6½	7	8
European	36	36½	37	37½	38	38½	39	39½	40	41
Men's suits										
British	36	38	40	42	44	46	48			
European	44	46	48	50	52	54	56			
Men's shirts										
British	14	15	15½	16	16½	17	17½	18		
European	36	38	40	41	42	43	44	45		
Men's shoes										
British	6	7	7½	8	8½	9	9½	10	11	12
European	39	40	41	42	42½	43	43½	44	45	46

It's worth trying on clothes and shoes first if you can, as some manufacturers don't adhere strictly to the European sizes.

Fig. 5. Clothing/shoe size conversions.

The Portuguese are very smart dressers, in all walks of life, and the range of shoes and quality clothing stores is vast, but at a price. However, as dress and appearance is so vital to these people it is worth remembering that if you intend to do business within Portuguese circles, or are taken out by Portuguese acquaintances, it pays to make a bit of effort. Men usually wear ties, but are not necessarily restricted to a suit, often a smart jacket will suffice; ladies tend to wear elegant clothing, again often with a jacket. There seems to be a national leaning towards subtle hues of brown and green, olive being particularly popular. Younger people, as everywhere, are happy in shorts or jeans.

The summer

The summer months in Portugal can be unbearably hot, so if your stay involves being there at this time, do take plenty of cotton clothing, especially white to deflect the sun, cool footwear, and a hat. You will find that journeys will leave you sticky and often soak your clothing, so have plenty of shirts and underwear – washing will dry overnight in this weather. In other parts of Portugal this time of the year is very much the same, and for going out at night a cardigan over the shoulders is more than adequate (more to keep the insects off you than to provide heat).

Autumn

Most places are still very warm, especially the Algarve, so again summer clothing will suffice, with woollens or jackets to take out in the evening. Lisbon is renowned for its river breezes so bear this in mind; if you set out on a warm afternoon it's very refreshing, but by mid-evening can feel rather cold.

Winter

Although December can still be warm in the Algarve, where some people have been on the beach on Christmas Day, elsewhere there is a noticeable drop in temperature. Do not be fooled into thinking the Algarve is always an ideal resting place due to its inviting sun, as January, February and even March can all be wet and miserable. This catches many people out so be prepared with warm clothing, waterproofs, suitable footwear and brollies. The same applies as you move northwards up the coast, and inland be prepared for freezing conditions – the Alentejo and far northern regions are notoriously cold in winter.

Spring

The first signs of summer re-appear with warming sunshine emerging in most regions so the clothing which suited autumn conditions will again be adequate. As the weeks progress you can start to peel off the layers.

Etiquette and respect
Don't enter any religious/official building scantily clad. If you must wear shorts, OK, but cover up bare shoulders, midriffs and chests. When dealing with administrative departments, you are far more likely to be taken seriously if you are covered up than standing discussing in shorts/ vest/flip-flops, however hot it might be outside.

PETS

The Portuguese have a very different attitude to domestic animals, as do most southern European countries, in that few people really have what could be termed 'family pets'. Dogs are usually working animals, or are kept chained up outside. Few people have cats, and rabbits are for consumption. Many people will have a small cage on the outside wall of their house, with canaries and other colourful little birds. In the Algarve, and in backstreets elsewhere, there are many 'street' dogs, who forage in bins and are fed by local butchers. They will not cause you any harm if you leave them alone and don't try to fuss them in the hot weather.

If you decide that you cannot bear to leave behind your own trusted companion, then you can take animals with you, but you must make sure they have all necessary inoculations before you go, including vaccination against rabies; check with your local vet about the Pet Passport scheme. You will also have to take with you proof of vaccinations and any other recent treatment. These will need to be translated into Portuguese and authorised by a competent vet. You may also require a special import licence from the Portuguese authorities. Check with the Consulate before you make any plans.

Travelling through France and Spain you must be careful not to let the animal out of your sight, as rabies is a problem there (so far Portugal seems to be rabies-free). In rural areas in Portugal you will have difficulties in the warm, damp months with irksome ticks (see Chapter 11). If you are transporting your pet by air advise the airline before travel and make sure you have all the relevant certificates to hand for boarding and arrival. On return to the UK you may need a licence to re-import your animal. For further information contact the Ministry of Agriculture, Fisheries and Food. See end matter for address.

CUSTOMS

If you have decided on a definite move your next thoughts should include what amount of your own household goods you wish to take with you. Of course if you only intend to move on a semi-permanent basis, perhaps retaining property in the UK to which you will return at a later date, then perhaps you only require your 'favourite' pieces of furniture removing. A complete house removal may cost on average £5,000. Further details can be obtained from any of the removal firms listed at the end of this book.

Before you leave

If you intend to set up your main residence in Portugal, you need to have your Residence Permit in order to prove you are importing goods for your own use, and qualify for duty-free importation. You also require a full inventory of all the items, and in the case of electricals include details such as serial numbers.

If you are only intending to stay in Portugal in your own holiday home, or second home, you can still import your effects duty-free on proof of property ownership (the deeds, or **escritura**), but you also have to prove you have owned the goods for at least three months.

It is vital that you have receipts/proof of purchase for your goods – bear this in mind before making packing arrangements. Make sure, too, that you have duplicate copies of your inventory – you will usually need one copy in Portuguese.

For goods transported by road, the EU relaxation on

border controls means that arrival in Portugal via another EU country should not be subject to any formal customs procedures. For effects arriving by sea or air, ensure you have all the relevant documentation – delays in producing this can add to your stress and you may face extra charges at customs.

On arrival

You will need to sign a declaration (**declaração**) stating that you will not sell, rent or transfer your goods for 12 months following the date of import. In the case of valuable works of art, rare items etc, this may be extended to up to ten years. There may be a charge imposed on your goods by customs to release them, based on weight and value.

Use a reputable agent to arrange your move, and seek clarification if unclear from the Consulate, or Lisbon Customs and Excise, Direcção Geral das Alfândegas, Rua Terreiro Trigo, 1100 Lisboa. Tel: 21-888 3576.

PREPARING FINANCIALLY/CULTURALLY

Finance

Any move or stay in another country can incur costs of one kind or other. If you are going for a short to medium stay you will have accommodation costs (hotel or rent), transport, tuition/course fees, domestic bills and everyday living costs. Although it is still relatively cheap on a daily basis to live in Portugal, you do need to plan ahead and budget for what you think you will spend. For a longer stay, in addition to the above costs, you may have expenses such as paying for residence permits, driving licences, insurance, deposits on rented accommodation and connection charges for domestic utilities. You may not necessarily find work immediately. Make sure you are covered for all eventualities, worse-case scenarios are a must.

Culture

Whatever your reason for visiting Portugal, even for a shorter-term holiday, it's not a bad idea to read about the place and its people before you go. There are many travel guides to the country, most giving background information on the history of the place and how it has moulded the people. Most good bookshops or libraries in the UK offer a range of books to choose from.

In addition, you really should try to learn some of the language in advance, even the pure basics – everyday greetings and pleasantries. Although Portuguese is a difficult language (despite looking like Spanish, it sounds more like Russian), you *can* pick up a smattering with a bit of effort. The best way to do this is to enrol on a short language course at your local college, where you will meet like-minded people intent on defying that age-old national stereotype of the loud Brit abroad! Some colleges run holiday language courses, usually for six to ten weeks, and these will give you enough to start communicating. I used to run combined language and culture courses, which proved very popular, especially when we got on to learning about Portuguese wine!

Portuguese is growing in popularity in this country, but not every area offers it as a course. If you have problems finding a course in your area, drop me a line c/o The Association for Language Learning, 150 Railway Terrace,

Rugby CV21 3HN, and I'll see how I can help. If you can't get onto a course the next best thing is to follow a coursebook with a tape. There are many learner-friendly courses around these days – see Further Reading section on p. 257. When you go to Portugal find a place in your packing for your book, tape and a phrase book and dictionary – continue your endeavours once out there.

HOW TO GET THERE

Having made the decision to get up and go, your next move will be to consider how to get yourself and your belongings over the waters, and this obviously depends very much on your intentions:

- How long will your stay be?
  - is this your definitive trip there?
  - is it an exploratory trip?
- How much will you need with you initially?
  - clothes and personal items
  - furniture
- Will you need a car with you?
- Are you working to a budget?
- Your exact destination
  - north/south
  - coast/inland
- Are you travelling alone/with family?

Air

This is by far the quickest, most efficient way to travel, especially if you have little baggage. Flights to Portugal depart from Manchester, Heathrow and Gatwick, and some of the smaller UK airports cover package flights to Faro. The main companies dealing specifically with UK–Portugal flights are BA, Tel: (020) 7897 4000 or individual branches, or Reservations on (0990) 224224, GO, which offers cheap, no-frills flights to Faro and Lisbon from Stansted Airport: (08456) 054231, TAP (Portuguese Airlines), 19 Regent Street, London SW1: Tel (020) 7828 0262, and Portugalia Airlines, Tel (0990) 502048. AB Airlines operate a scheduled flight from Gatwick to Lisbon, Tel: (0345) 464748.

There are of course many charter flights to Faro in the summer, along with package deals, which sometimes offer a cheaper way to get yourself out there in the first place. On offer over the winter are cheap long-stay holidays, designed for those wishing to escape the British winter blues, but certainly affording an ideal opportunity to reach your destination: they provide cheap, good accommodation in large hotel complexes whilst you look around for alternatives. I chose this option on one visit to the Algarve, and ended up paying the equivalent of about £20 a week for the lovely apartment I was in (including gas, water and electricity) over the winter until I moved on. Caravela, a subsidiary of TAP, offers special package deals: 38–44 Gillingham Street, 3rd Floor, London SW1V 1JW. Tel: (020) 7630 9223.

Ask at your local travel agent for other long-stay deals or contact the Portuguese Trade and Tourism Office (ICEP) for more information on travel to Portugal, Tel: (020) 7494 1441 (www.portugalinsite.pt). They have a comprehensive Tour Operators Guide, updated annually.

Student travel agencies often have bargain flights and you don't always have to be a student to qualify. Try STA travel (most university campuses), London branch on (020) 7361 6161, or Campus Travel on (020) 7730 3402.

Ferry

If you are taking your car you have a couple of alternative boat routes:

♦ To a French port such as St Malo or Caen, and drive to Portugal, about 1,100 miles, or ferry/shuttle and motor rail from Paris to Lisbon.

♦ To Santander or Bilbao, N. Spain: 24-hour crossing and drive to Portugal, about 550 miles.

Contact Brittany Ferries (Santander or via France), Tel: (0990) 360 360. P&O Ferries (for Bilbao): Tel: (0990) 980980. The latest leaflet will be available from travel agents.

Costs vary according to season, number of passengers travelling in vehicle, size of vehicle. The ferries may not be operating during certain winter months, so check in advance before planning your journey.

Information
Le Shuttle, Tel: (0990) 353535.
French railways (for motor rail), 179 Piccadilly, London W1. Tel: (020) 7499 9333.

Trains

A marvellous journey for the more adventurous is by train. Take Eurostar from London to Paris and then trains to Portugal via Irun/Hendaye (the 'Sud-Express' Paris to Pampilhosa), travel time London – Lisbon about 1 ½ days. I have twice done the journey back from Lisbon by train and providing you can put up with a lack of home comforts for a while, particularly when you change trains at the Spanish and Portuguese borders, it's a great opportunity to travel with a wide variety of people. I was lucky once to be in a compartment with a Portuguese family who shared their fruit/cheese and wine with me, and kept an eye on my luggage when I needed to stretch my legs. The only drawback is the lack of hygienic conditions in the loos, which do deteriorate when you transfer from the French train at the border.

Information

Eurostar: Waterloo Station, London, and all main BR stations. Tel: (01233) 617575.

BR Continental Section: Victoria Station, London SW1. Tel: (020) 7834 2345.

Portuguese Rail Timetable: BAS Overseas Publications Ltd, 48–50 Sheen Lane, London SW14 8LQ.

Coaches

Coaches can be caught from/to Algarve/Lisbon/Oporto and the main cities in between via Spain and France. The journey, though, can be debilitating and not to be recommended for everyone, especially in the stifling summer months. Travel time for London Victoria – Algarve is about 2 ½ days. Frequent food stops are made but these are invariably at pricey watering holes where the driver gets free food for taking coachloads of passengers there. Pack your own food if at all possible, and take plenty to drink. The journey I made this way from Portimão (Algarve) to

London was initially on a French coach that allowed smoking but banned eating, and drove so erratically that one poor lady was ill all the way to northern Spain. What a joy it was in Paris to swap to an English National Express coach. I have also travelled home from Bragança in northern Portugal, on a packed coach, and whilst it is invariably a cheap option to get back, it does have its drawbacks.

In Paris the second leg of the journey may depart from a different bus station and usually no help is given to transfer you there. Watch out for rip-off taxis. Travel as a group if you can, or use the underground. On my arrival in London I discovered that my legs had bloated to twice their normal size due to the length of time sitting in one position, and the air conditioning inside the coach, so do be careful.

It may be worth checking with your GP before you travel to make sure you are not likely to be prone to problems with blood pressure or circulation.

Information

Eurolines (National Express): Victoria Coach Station, Buckingham Palace Road, London SW1. Tel: (020) 7730 0202.

ONWARD TRAVEL

Airports

Arriving at an airport in Portugal is like any other airport you may have passed through, albeit on a smaller scale than some. There are three international airports, Oporto, Lisbon and Faro, in the Algarve. Lisbon deals with both business and tourist clients visiting the capital and surrounding areas. It has recently expanded considerably, mostly in response to extra demand during the Expo 98 exhibition, but also through the rise in popularity of Lisbon for short breaks. Oporto serves the traditional industrial north, and Faro almost exclusively caters for visitors to the Algarve, although I have frequently found it cheaper to fly to Faro and travel northwards by rail or coach.

On arrival you still pass through the conventional Passport Control, so keep your passport handy in case any query should arise. You will find, though, that you are waved through without so much as a glance at your ID. A friendly hello (*Bom dia/boa tarde/boa noite*) and thank you (*obrigado/a*) will show that you are not another 'typical tourist' with ignorance of the language. Display the common courtesies you might expect yourself. From Passport Control you will need to collect your belongings (**bagagem**) and then go through customs (**Alfândega**). Again, you are highly unlikely to be stopped now, so long as you appear to be carrying only the normal personal effects (camera, radio, sports equipment). If you are awaiting imported household goods, you should approach an official with the documents mentioned earlier.

Signs to look out for in the airport

Recolha de bagagem	baggage reclaim	Alfândega	Customs
Café/restaurante	food places (often pay first before you see the food)	Vôos internacionais	international flights
		Nada a declarar	nothing to declare
Serviços senhoras	ladies WC	Cavalheiros	gents WC
Aluguel (carros)	car rental	Câmbio	exchange
Correios	stamps	Entrada	entry
Saída	exit	Chegadas	arrivals .
Partidas	departures	Vôos domésticos	domestic flights

Getting to your final destination

Once through the hassle of arriving, the next stage of your adventure is to reach your internal destination. Travel itself is dealt with in more detail later in this book. Should you arrive at a ferry terminal your choice may be rail/coach or you may arrange car hire at the terminal itself. However, as most people will probably be arriving by air, let us examine the possibilities.

Bus

In Lisbon and Oporto a bus service, Linha Verde, Green Line, runs between the airport and a main train station (Santa Apolônia in Lisbon and Campolide in Oporto), with stop-off points all along the way. If you need to travel on after arrival this is the easiest way, as you can get into the city centres without the push and shove of normal, busy service buses. There can be nothing worse than trying to get yourself and all your belongings onto and along a packed bus! There are some town buses whose routes take them via the airport but unless you really know where you have to go, try to avoid them or you may end up at the opposite end of the city to where you intended. Pay the driver as you get on – you will probably want either the station (**a estação**) or city centre (**o centro**).

Taxi

Don't be under any illusion – taxi-drivers the world over are notorious for swindling unsuspecting tourists so you may as well be prepared to be conned. Taxis, spacious black and green or buff-coloured old Mercedes, travel like the wind and can provide an exhilarating spin through the crowded streets. Within cities there should be a meter, but for longer distances a charge is made per km so you can always check beforehand to get an estimate of cost. Also at the **Informações** in the airports there is now a list of approximate prices for certain destinations, and anyone trying to overcharge can, theoretically, be reported. Charges can increase dramatically after 10pm, on average by about 20%. It is customary to tip, usually about 10%, use your own discretion; some drivers may stand and watch you struggle to put your bags in the boot, I rarely tip this kind. It pays to be able to speak some of the language, as you are less likely to be conned if you appear to know what's what.

Rail

You will need to catch a taxi to the nearest station and from there on rail is relatively trouble-free. However, there was a spate of foreign travellers being manhandled and thrown off trains for not having a ticket. Train travel is so cheap it's not worth trying to evade payment: if you are in a rush to get on a train that is due to leave, try to gesture to someone that you want to get a ticket and could they help you.

Car

You may have prearranged car hire or you can always hire on arrival, with a wide choice of firms, all the reps speaking English. Or of course you may have travelled to Portugal in your own car.

For further details see Chapter 9 on driving.

CHECKLIST

1. Do you have all the necessary documentation to allow you to visit and import your household goods?

2. Have you thought about what clothing and other items you will need there?

3. Has your pet had relevant vaccinations?

4. Have you planned out your finances for survival, with worse-case scenarios in mind?

5. Have you read about the country and its people in anticipation of life there?

6. Have you planned your travel, and have tickets and itineraries organised, including onward travel on arrival?

Accommodation

GUEST HOUSES AND HOTELS

The choice is fairly wide, with quality and prices to suit all tastes, whether you are spending a couple of weeks travelling around looking for a more permanent location, waiting for your own property to be completed or constantly moving around. Most towns have a few larger hotels (**hotéis**), starred ★ as in the UK, with a variety of other possibilities. Don't be surprised if conditions in some are not quite as you might wish. Use your common sense — a few glances around a neighbourhood will identify possible dens of iniquity to avoid. If you are desperate for a night's sleep and find yourself in a suspicious place, lock your door and leave the key in the lock. Block your ears to strange comings and goings! You may also need to make do with a strip wash in the morning, with only a sink in the room, and even the *Yellow Pages* for loo paper. Be prepared to be eyed suspiciously as you emerge from the dingy doorway onto a sunny street the next morning. Not for the faint-hearted, but a real experience, and very cheap – I stayed in an establishment like this in Oporto, with my husband for £5 a night in 2001.

Available accommodation

Pousada — State-run system. Hotels in historic locations (such as castles or monasteries), or areas of natural beauty. Usually pricey, with a ranking of categories, depending on location, season, type of building and region. Good value in low season if you fancy staying in a sumptuous environment. Contact: Enatur, Av. Santa Joana Princesa 10A, 1700 Lisbon. Tel: 351-21-8442001, or http://www.pousadas.pt The Portuguese Tourism Office also has details.

Estalagem — Inn. Quality hotel, though not necessarily expensive. Usually has a restaurant.

Manor house — Predominantly in the Minho region of northern Portugal. You stay as a private guest in some of the loveliest country houses imaginable. Contact: Turismo de Ponte de Lima, Praça da República, 4990 Ponte de Lima.

Hotéis — As mentioned previously, one- to five-star. Prices range from about £12 for an en-suite double room with breakfast.

Pensão — B&B. Can vary in quality, generally cheaper than hotel, usually breakfast only.

Residência/residencial — Similar to pensão.

Youth hostel — Although mostly still quite basic, they are an ideal cheap stop-over place, and great for young people/students/itinerant travellers. You need a YHA card issued in the UK.
Contact: Movijovem (who manage the hostels), Av. Duque de Ávila, 137 1050, Lisbon. Tel: 21-355-9081.

Camping — See Chapter 9 on driving.

FINDING RENTED ACCOMMODATION

Your search for rented accommodation could start in the UK. Many daily/weekly publications, both journals and magazines, hold ads for private rented villas, the majority of which are situated in the Algarve. Usually, however, these will be short term and, as they are designed more for large groups sharing costs, pound for pound they will probably be an expensive option; however, if all else fails it is at least one avenue you could explore.

Once on Portuguese land the hunt should be easier. Again your main lead could be via the local journals, both English and Portuguese. If you envisage a language problem your choice is limited to what's on offer from the, mainly, ex-pat community. Ask around in bars, and keep a look-out for signs. In the Portuguese sector there will be a far wider choice, particularly in tourist areas, and you should turn to the journal pages marked **CLASSIFICADOS : imobiliário : ALUGA-SE**, for rent. Interpreting the ads can sometimes be a problem; typical ones might read as in Figures 6 and 7.

Prices may range from approximately £50 per week for a small non-furnished flat to £500 per week for luxury apartments in parts of Lisbon and Oporto. Remember they will mostly be apartments unless you venture out to country regions.

Another source of renting is via an estate agent, and certainly the tourist areas are teeming with ex-pat-run businesses which can give you advice and sort out any

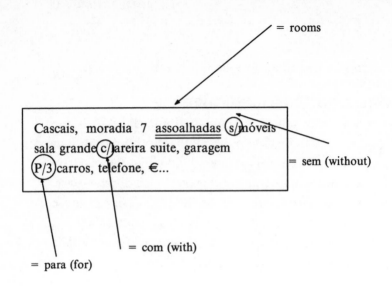

Fig 6. Accommodation for rent: advertisement 1.

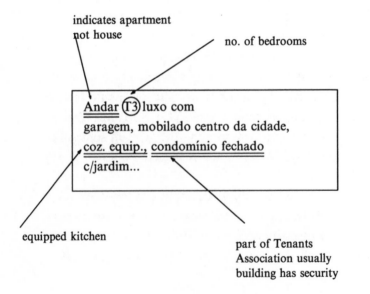

Fig. 7. Accommodation for rent: advertisement 2.

administrative work. A relocation agency can save you time by searching out property to a brief given by you, but it is a costly way to proceed.

Word of mouth is one of the best means of finding a bargain through friends, colleagues, school contacts – and often the local Tourism offices have leads you can follow up – it really pays to talk to people.

RENT LAWS

There has long been concern in Portugal that the law concerning tenants has been heavily weighted in favour of those tenants, however short their stay may be. With outdated contracts which fixed many rents at an incredibly low rate, and in most cases a minimum rental period of five years, it has not been an easy option for Portuguese landlords to rent out their property. The fear of not being able to get rid of unwelcome visitors and lack of funding to improve their property have led to a wariness when it comes to this accommodation sector. The government introduced a new initiative to encourage landlords to rent out, by not levying income tax on rental income, but although you may find plenty of choice in the large cities, smaller areas may still prove difficult, and in larger cities rental prices have been pushed skywards through prime properties being taken over by embassies and international companies.

Tourist regions – Here new laws govern rental contracts, as in most cases the letting will be a straightforward short-term holiday let. As long as a contract clearly states the rental period, and is for temporary occupation only, and in an area where limited stay would be the norm, both parties should have no problems.

As in all agreements of this type, it is worth checking details first with an expert in the subject. Ask one of the estate agents to go over the contract with you and make sure you have copies of all relevant documents for your own reference. For example, make sure you know who is responsible for the domestic bills – are these included in the rental? Check the property for damp (a big problem in Portugal) – will the landlord supply dehumidifiers (and is there sufficient power to run them?). Clarify who is responsible for general repairs, and are you happy with the security? Have meters read before you move in, and check where you obtain gas bottles (if appropriate) and what the arrangements for rubbish removal are. Make an inventory of furniture and its condition and decide how the rent is to be paid – will it be collected or should it be paid to an agent? Keep receipts for everything. You may need someone to act as guarantor (**fiador**), and it is common to pay a security deposit plus two months' rent in advance.

ACCOMMODATION WITH FAMILIES

This is an ideal option for young people, perhaps those staying for a short time or those studying. The trauma of dislocating oneself from one's family, uprooting to foreign soil, and language difficulties add to the already hectic time of settling into a new classroom environment. Sharing life with a Portuguese family can therefore be reassuring and comforting.

Most families will have at least one English speaker in them, so until you are proficient with the language at least you'll get by – it is a great motivation to learn the language if you are obliged to speak it in the home. You'll learn more quickly, especially if visits to grandparents at first involve much smiling and jovial banter centred around you, which leaves you completely mystified. Portuguese family life is much more unified than that in the UK, with great respect for parents, grandparents and young children. Weekends usually involve big family visits with lots of wonderful food – in all of which you will be included.

Problems of living with a family

These only really arise when perhaps you want to go out with classmates and come in late, but a warning beforehand to your family will smooth things over. If they are anything like the family I stayed with on my first visit they may give you a key, providing you don't wake up the neighbourhood at 5 am. Staying with a family is an ideal introduction into Portuguese life and especially valuable to a young person on their own who has not travelled much before, and is particularly reassuring to worried parents left behind in the UK. I would heartily recommend it, as my stays with Carmen, my 'Portuguese mum' as she became known, gave me a valuable insight into their culture.

Finding a family

Families are usually found through personal contacts. Ask friends and colleagues if they know any respectable families, and write to them (in Portuguese if you can), asking for help with accommodation. Offer to pay a daily rate, and send some information about yourself with a photo.

If for some reason you find you don't get on with the family, and can't work out the problem, then it's a case of moving on and trying somewhere else, but as Portuguese hospitality is well-known, these kinds of problems are rare. Where they do exist, they can be of your own making!

BUYING. . .

If you have found property you have decided on as a permanent dwelling, you then face a drawn-out, complicated procedure to allow you to purchase it. However, with the right advice from either a UK-based or offshore financial institution, or a legally recognised and authorised agent in Portugal (**mediador autorizado**), the process can be made infinitely less troublesome, and most people survive unscathed.

Finance

This can be raised in various ways, including secured loans on property, as in the UK, purchasing through shares in an offshore company, or remortgaging existing property in the UK.

In March 2002, the Portuguese authorities committed themselves to a new law targeting offshore companies, in an attempt to combat a rising level of fiscal abuse, including money laundering. Tax implications are involved, and this way of raising capital looks increasingly less desirable.

Every individual case will be different and you should consult one of the property/finance agents listed in the contacts list for clearer details relating to your own situation.

A clear and useful publication on all aspects of property and finance in Portugal is *Buying a Home in Portugal* by David Hampshire, published by Survival Books.

Main stages in the process

The contract
The process begins with the legally binding promissory contract (for both parties): The **Contrato de Promessa de Compra e Venda**. You may have to pay a 10% deposit, which will be forfeited if you back out. Should the vendor default they must repay the buyer twice the original deposit.

Foreign funds — **Boletim de Autorização de Capitais privados**. You no longer need the authority of the Bank of Portugal to import foreign funds to purchase your property, but you are supposed to notify the Bank if you are a nonresident (for statistical purposes).

Transfer tax – **SISA**. Property rates vary depending on type, location and age, and with annual changes in the rate, you should check first with your adviser.

Deed – **Escritura**, the official property deed for you. This must be signed at the **Notários** office by all parties, all information having been verified beforehand.

Land registry. You must register the property at the local **Conservatória** (Land Registry) and check the description in the Register matches exactly the position on the ground – any discrepancy could lead to later boundary disputes, and the **Repartição de Finanças** (Inland Revenue offices).

You must also register yourself at the tax office for payment of rates (**contribuição predial**).

Your legal and financial advisers will assist you all the way, and lead you through the maze of documentation and jargon, carrying out land searches for you, as at home, and applying for your tax number and even, should you require it, be given the power of attorney to sign all necessary documents for you. Don't try to undertake it yourself, even with perfect Portuguese; it's a tricky process and you can very easily come unstuck.

...AND SELLING

If you have property to sell in Portugal, be it residential or business, the emphasis is once more upon a fully licensed agent carrying out the transactions for you. It may be that you have returned to the UK and have to place your property and legal work in the hands of a third party. Working this way, from a distance, is never ideal, but is possible and many people have successfully done so. In the contacts list you will find a list of property agents and legal firms, both Portuguese and English, working in both countries, and your first step should be to seek advice from one (or more) of them.

The process

This follows very much the same lines as for purchase of a property, except of course as the vendor you will have certain taxes to pay on your sale.

♦ Find a reputable, authorised property agent, and when a buyer is found seek proper legal advice.

- Make sure you are in possession of all documentation relating to the property, especially title deeds; all these should be passed on via your solicitor to the purchaser's solicitor.

- On signing the **promissory contract**, remember that in the event of your backing out, you will be obliged to repay the purchaser twice the original deposit. Therefore you must be very sure at this stage that you intend to proceed.

- Capital gains – a trip to your local tax department (**Finanças**) will reveal what you are expected to pay (see next section).

- Finally the **Escritura** (deed of transfer) is signed in the presence of the Public Notary.

PROPERTY TAXES
Whether buying or selling you will end up paying taxes on property somewhere along the line, so do bear this in mind when organising your finances.

SISA (purchase tax)

Land for development	10% purchase price
Land for rustic purposes	8% purchase price
Residential property:	a scale from 0–26% purchase price

Municipal Tax and VAT
There is also a Municipal tax (**contribução autarquia**) on both land and buildings, and VAT (**IVA**) on services such as building contracts. Your legal advisers should check these for you.

IRS (Income Tax)

Imposto sobre o rendimento das pessoas singulares is payable by all residents of Portugal (nationals or otherwise), due on worldwide income, and non-residents on their Portuguese source of income. If you have been in Portugal more than 183 days in any calendar year, or have residential accommodation there, you will be deemed a resident. IRS is payable on sale of property but there are certain conditions for exemptions, for example if you reinvest the money in more property.

Double taxation
Portugal and UK have an agreement in this respect to avoid tax on capital gains being paid twice. A credit system is used so that if you are a UK resident for tax purposes, and pay capital gains tax to the Inland Revenue on the sale of your property in Portugal, a credit will be issued to balance any tax paid to the Portuguese tax authorities for the same reason.

BUILDING YOUR OWN PLACE

For many years now there has existed the romantic notion of selling up, moving abroad and seeing life reconstructed as you work together as a family to build your new home. In many cases this idea has been followed through, and successfully so. But for every success story, and even those tinged with many a minor hitch, there will be told the equally sad tale of how it all went wrong. Lack of communication with hired builders, plans designed inadequately, proper inspection of land and drainage not carried out, lack of foresight as to the surrounding area and its usage present and future – all of these and other problems can leave you with a headache, a lot of legal wrangling, and ultimately, sorrow. So, if you still want your own property built, how can these problems be avoided?

Once you have found a piece of land adequate for your purposes, as always working through a reputable agent, have it thoroughly checked out in many respects:

◆ **Legal ownership** – do you have the right to build on it? Check for restrictions. Does anyone else, for example a farmer have a claim on it? Check farming boundaries.

◆ **Physical inspection** – water supply/supply of electricity and phone lines/adequate drain facilities/subsidence/ flooding.

◆ **Planning** – thoroughly check official permission. Double-check plans are exactly as you want them. Make sure any fees are paid (for example to planning department).

◆ **Building** – if you employ mostly Portuguese workers, ensure there is no language barrier, otherwise instructions may be ignored and problems arise.

Check supply of materials and make sure you know who is paying for them. If you ask for cavity walls make sure you get them! You will need a fossa (sewage pit) – make sure you have and it's in the right place. Unfortunately building a house involves constant checking up on the process, so be prepared for toing and froing. The Consular Section of the British Embassy in Lisbon has further guidance on the pitfalls of purchasing land and having property built. See Useful Contacts for address.

LAWS AND RESTRICTIONS

When buying the land in the first place, you will be subject to the same legal and financial process as for buying an existing property. The land must be checked out for legal ownership through searches, and the process of paying a deposit, raising finance, contracts and taxes follows the same lines as before. Don't forget there will be SISA (purchase tax) of approximately 10% purchase price, to pay on the land. You would be well advised to have a legal expert guide you through the pitfalls.

One important factor in relation particularly to building is the recent legislation regarding restrictions, especially in the Algarve, where it was decided that the rate of rapid urban development had to be curbed. The **PROTAL** (Plano Regional de Ordenamento do Território do Algarve) laws in force there will not allow any construction on certain plots of land unless there was prior permission granted on that land. It would be wise to investigate before you start digging. Elsewhere in Portugal you may find similar Regional plans now in place. You may need to seek confirmation that the planned property is compatible with the Regional plan.

Other restrictions on land and property purchase mean that permission must be sought from the Portuguese External Commerce Institute (ICEP). These include cases such as:

- If you have three other properties elsewhere in Portugal

- If you want to purchase office/industrial accommodation

◆ If you have property(ies) with more than 500m^2 of covered-in area.

Be sure of your legal position by checking first.

TIMESHARE

Much has been spoken about timeshare and its charms and its snares. In Portugal laws over the last decade have made timeshare touting openly on the streets illegal, but laws are still being flouted. Most people will recognise the sheer inconvenience and irritation of being attacked whilst strolling along a promenade, and persuaded to attend a showing of an apartment. These OPCs (outside personal contacts) are a public nuisance but, like it or not, timeshare is very much part of the property industry and many people do choose it as an option for staying in countries like Portugal.

Is there a reputable timeshare company? Obviously there must be or so many people would not consider it as a means of accommodation, but the horror stories of things going wrong are numerous and caution should certainly be the operative policy here. Recommendations from friends and relatives are one of the best ways of judging here, and never be too keen to part with any money, such as a deposit, until you are satisfied with exactly what you are being offered.

Remember also that timeshare only offers you a short period of annual accommodation, so should not be on your list of options for permanent residence. The pros and cons are many, and one of the clearest guides to the subject is included in the publication by Rosemary de Rougement

Buying Property in Portugal, pp. 44–48.

CHECKLIST

1. Do you know what kind of property you are looking for?

2. Have you checked the property thoroughly?

3. Is the contract clear about responsibilities? (Are you?)

4. Have you sought legal/financial advice on buying property?

5. Are you sure about which taxes you will need to pay, and have you budgeted for them?

6. Have you thoroughly checked planning and building regulations?

(4)

Domestic Life

REGISTERING AT THE EMBASSY/CONSULATE

Although it is not a legal requirement to register with your country's Embassy or Consulate, if you are going to spend any time in Portugal it is a good idea to do so. In the (highly unlikely) event of military action, natural disaster or other turmoil, the consular staff can get hold of you more easily and ensure your safety. Equally, should family in the UK be trying to reach you in the case of an emergency, the process can be speeded up if your whereabouts are known. Registration cards will require you to present your passport, fill in some forms and pay a small fee.

In addition to this, consular staff can give you advice and information on applying for your Residence Permit and driving licence and give guidance on administrative matters. It is also where you can obtain advice on what to do if there is a death in the family, or if a seriously ill person needs urgent repatriation.

Like all government officials, the consular staff can often be pretty busy and may not always be the most welcoming of people. Be tolerant and patient! The British Consulates in Portugal are:

British Embassy (Consular section), Rua de São Bernardo 33, 1200 Lisboa. Tel: 21-392 4160. Fax: 21-392 4188.

British Consulate, Avenida da Boavista 3072, 4100 Porto. Tel: 22-618 4789. Fax: 22-610 0438.

British Consulate, Largo Francisco A Mauricio, 7–1, 8500 Portimão. Tel: 282-417800/417804. Fax: 282-417806.

OBTAINING A RESIDENCY PERMIT

You do not need to apply for this before you enter Portugal, and if your stay is for less than three months (even if you will be working), or if you will be undertaking seasonal work which does not exceed eight months, you do not need a resident's permit. However, you will need either a temporary or permanent residency permit if your stay is for longer. Permits vary in category but all can be renewed and extended. Spouses of people going there to work also require a permit and children of under 14 may have their names endorsed on their parents' permit.

In all cases you need to pay a visit to your nearest Foreigners Service (**Serviço dos Estrangeiros e Fronteiras**) – be prepared and take all the necessary paperwork listed below. But be warned, regulations may change and you should not expect to manage everything successfully in one visit (it never works that way in Portuguese officialdom). Allow plenty of time: bureaucracy is slow and queues are generally long.

> **What you need to obtain your Cartão de Residência**
>
> **As an employee:**
> - **Two photocopies of each page of your passport.**
> - **Three colour passport-size photos.**
> - **Declaration from your company/organisation stating your contract details.**
>
> **You may also require evidence of a health certificate.**

Self-employed people need to provide details of their work or business. People of independent means (including the retired) need to produce evidence that they can support themselves and their dependants without state assistance.

As a dependant:

- Two photocopies of each page of your passport.

- Three colour passport photos.

- Two copies of your marriage certificate (if appropriate).

- Two copies of your spouse's Residency Permit, if already obtained.

- Two copies of a letter from your spouse's company, stating s/he has a contract to work.

- Two copies of a letter from your spouse stating s/he will be financially responsible for you.

Non-EU citizens require a visa which should have been obtained from the Portuguese consulate in their own

---

country. For children you also require two copies of their birth certificates.

Once you have filled in the relevant forms you will be given a receipt (keep this safe), and eventually you will be informed that your Cartão is ready to pick up. To collect it you need the receipt and a small fee.

Your Residency Permit will be your official ID card in Portugal. You will be required to carry it with you at all times. Until you obtain one your passport is your only ID.

The main offices of the Borders and Aliens (Foreigners) service are located at:

Head Office – Rua Cons. José Silvestre Ribeiro 4, 1600 Lisboa. Tel: 21-711 5000.
Linha Azul (Information Line): 21-715 5628/715 5270.
Regional Offices:
Av. António Augusto de Aguiar 20, 1000 Lisboa. Tel: 21-3143112.
Rua D João IV, 536, Apart. 4819, 4013 Porto Codex. Tel: 22-5104308.
Rua Venâncio Rodrigues, 25-31, 3000 Coimbra. Tel: 239-824045.
Rua Dr José de Matos, 14, 8000 Faro. Tel: 289-805822.

CURRENCY

The Euro

Portugal joined the European Monetary Union on 1 January 1999, and officially its fiscal currency is now the Euro.

Get hold of a selection of notes and coins before you leave the UK and familiarise yourself with them. Make yourself an approximate personal conversion chart to help you get used to what things cost when you arrive. You'll find that after living there for a while you no longer need mentally to compare costs – you'll be aware of what things ought to cost in relation to your new environment itself.

Credit cards
Standard cards are generally widely accepted, with Visa the most common. You can withdraw cash from the Multibanco cash machines. Check with your own card issuer first to see if they levy a fee for these transactions.

LEARNING THE LANGUAGE
As mentioned in Chapter 2, it is really essential that you try to learn even the basics of Portuguese before you go. Although you may be heading for a mainly ex-pat area, and many Portuguese people speak very good English, you ought to be aware of what is going on around you. When you make the effort a whole new world opens up to you, from conversing simply about your purchases at the market, to understanding legal documents and socialising with new Portuguese friends.

Hopefully you will have taken my earlier advice and started some Portuguese before you arrive in Portugal. Once you get there, there are many other things you can do to continue the good work and gain confidence, either formally or for yourself.

◆ Enrol on a course at a language school or college –
look in the *Yellow Pages* (*Páginas Amarelas*) for details
(see also Chapter 10).

◆ Look out for private lessons, or English/Portuguese
conversation exchanges advertised in papers, church
and school newsletters, or even bars.

◆ Start to read in Portuguese – begin with a magazine of
some interest, or a women's, or general-interest magazine. Keep your expectations low to start with – small
paragraphs before double-page spreads.

◆ Watch TV – yes, it really *is* good for you! You may find
it very fast to start with, but you can at least get used to
the sound of the language. Programmes with English
subtitles can be useful, although they are not always totally accurate translations.

◆ Play Portuguese radio when you are at home.

Slowly but surely you will gain confidence if you try.
Don't be afraid of making mistakes – the Portuguese people will help you if you make an effort. Don't end up as
one of those ex-pats who live abroad for 20 years and
never utter more than a couple of words of the local language – unfortunately they do still exist!

ADJUSTING TO A NEW LIFESTYLE

Moving to a new location is always daunting as there are
so many factors to get used to: new workplace, home, different shops and facilities, unfamiliar surroundings and
making friends. Moving to a new country is exactly the
same, with the added worry of new customs and attitudes,
language, currency etc. One thing on your side in Portugal

is that the Portuguese people are very friendly and generally very willing to help newcomers fit in.

You do need to give yourself time to adjust – soak up the atmosphere, walk around and familiarise yourself with the locality, visit all the local facilities and introduce yourself to neighbours. The working day may be different from what you're used to, with shop opening hours different, and longer lunchtimes. If you are working you may find a different approach to the timetable, or working practices (see also next chapter). You may find, for example, that many more people than back home employ the services of a cleaning lady/daily help (**empregada**). It is quite normal practice and even people of moderate means do so.

Work, and social, etiquette have to be got used to and the only way to do it with any modicum of success is to throw yourself into taking on board how the locals live and behave. If you are shy, or reticent by nature, of course it's not going to be easy to start with. But in time, by going to places where you can meet locals (even if it's just a regular coffee at a certain café-bar), you'll begin to discover that you *can* integrate into the Portuguese lifestyle – if you allow yourself. If you still need the prop of the ex-pat community, find out where they hold events – the English papers in Portugal have listings, and schools, churches and bookshops often have details (see also Regional Directory). Having access to fellow-compatriots can be reassuring and comforting, but rely on them too much and you will certainly miss out on much of what Portuguese society has to offer. If you are heading for Lisbon or Oporto you may be interested in the following organisations, which also produce very useful publications offering a range of advice on daily life:

♦ International Women in Portugal, Apartado 1060, 2750 Cascais, Portugal. Publishes 'Feeling at Home in Portugal', a practical guide for foreign residents in Portugal. Also has a monthly newsletter called *A Janela*. The club hosts various events and activities.

♦ The Porto Mothers' Group, contact Zoe Harrap, Rua Luís de Camões 263, Miramar, 4405-088 Arcozelo VNG, Portugal. Publishes *Welcome to Porto*, a guide for expatriates.

SHOPPING

You will find that, apart from in the larger cities, the variety of shops available will be less than you may be used to, but you should still be able to satisfy all your basic requirements, leaving more adventurous shopping trips to days out in the city. More and more supermarket chains, such as the Brazilian chain Pão de Açúcar, Pingo Doce, Carrefour and Prisunic, are spreading across the country, but it is still a delight to do one's grocery shopping at traditional bakers, butchers and markets. Remember that the supermarket is an easy option language-wise, as you do not need to communicate with anyone; the smaller shop is a challenge you must meet.

As far as service is concerned, unfortunately the Portuguese are yet to discover that carrying on a conversation in front of an anxious-looking customer, reading a paper or idly gossiping with friends, have a detrimental effect on potential clients. A polite 'faz favor' may catch their attention, but don't expect them to leap over to you, face awash with an eager smile – that customer care treatment has, in many places, yet to be imported. But they are, if anything, courteous in their address.

On a practical level, shops are usually open (**aberto**) from 9 am to 1 pm and 3 pm to 7 pm in the afternoon. Most are closed (**fechado/encerrado**) on Saturday afternoons, some all day. The large shopping complexes are often open much longer hours, including weekends. Shops you may need include:

o talho	butcher	a padaria	bakery
o supermercado	supermarket	a sapataria	shoeshop
a papelaria	stationers	a livraria	bookshop
a farmácia	chemist	a mercearia	grocer's

As mentioned earlier be aware of all those extra days when the country grinds to a halt for religious and state holidays.

Bacon – Portuguese bacon is stringy and thin cut. If you buy Danish, it is usually cut very thick, and already expensive as an import, you end up paying almost for steaks of it.

Tea – take your own.

Supermarket trolleys are outside; you need a coin to release one. Often inside you have to leave your bags at the entrance and retrieve them later. At the fruit and veg section you need to know the names of the items in order to weigh them properly on the electronic scales; take a list of translations until you are familiar with them all. In many shops the goods you are buying will be wrapped at one counter whilst you take a ticket to the cashier, pay, then return with a receipt to pick up your parcel.

MARKETS

The market (**o mercado**) is an exciting and colourful part of Portuguese life, and even culture. Each town has its own permanent indoor fruit-veg market open each day from first light until about 5 or 6 pm. Many are also the location of the fish sellers, and include some butchers' units. Without exception all are lively places to visit and the choice of products is excellent, with prices even better. If you don't know the names of the products you require (especially tricky with the fish – some of which we don't have in the UK), then simply point and remember food is sold in kilos so be prepared to convert your pound of tomatoes to approximately ½ kilo (1k = 2.2lb). In addition to the daily market, once a week people will bring in other produce from the surrounding areas, and the stalls overflow onto the pavements where a myriad of sights, sounds and smells can send your senses reeling.

The obvious difference from our own markets is the sale of live produce; rabbits, chickens and other wildfowl are all available to the housewife. Be prepared for sights such as ten or twelve birds confined in a small cage in the searing heat. It may seem cruel to us. To the Portuguese it's merely a way of life and a way of life deeply connected with the land (**a terra**), so it does no good spouting animal rights, they simply won't comprehend.

There are also monthly travelling markets, or **feiras**, whose arrival is heralded often with the excitement of a circus or fair. In the main, the stallholders are itinerant gypsy families who move from town to town. Bargains can be found in clothing, bags, linen items, domestic goods, but you'll have to barter, and it takes a clever person to outwit the vendors. Do be careful with your purse/handbag when wandering around these places. If possible have your money inside a zipped or buttoned pocket on your person. Happy shopping.

TYPICAL FOOD

Portugal is an ideal place to eat, drink and be merry! You can choose from a wide spread of delicious, home-baked dishes, many of which are healthy and fulfilling. You can also follow the Portuguese and indulge in some of the most exquisite, sugar-loaded sweet goodies, and forget the waistline, and the dentist. Although most regions have their own special dish some meals are common to the whole land.

Soup

Not to be missed are the substantial soups (**sopas**), many made with potato purée and very wholesome; try the caldo verde, made from shredded kale.

Meat

For main meals typical meat dishes may include:

carne de porco à alentejana	pork with clams
leitão assado	roast sucking pig
bife de porco/de vaca	pork/beef steak

tripas à moda do Porto	Oporto-style tripe
fígado com arroz	liver with rice
feijoada	bean stew with black pudding

Fish

And for fish, the famous bacalhau (salted cod fish) is available in a variety of ways. Other popular fish dishes are:

lulas fritas	grilled squid
bacalhau à brás	cod fish with eggs and potatoes
arroz de marisco	seafood rice
pescada	hake
sardinhas assadas	grilled sardines
caldeirada	fish stew

Unfortunately most restaurants do seem to serve chips with a lot of dishes, although you are more likely to get boiled potatoes with fish. However, you can always order a tasty side salad (**uma salada mista**) to go with your meal instead.

Desserts

These include chocolate mousse, almond cake, fruit or ice cream, and if your teeth are up to it, try the delicious **doce de ovos**, made from eggs and sugar.

Meals

The Portuguese don't often eat a breakfast (**pequeno-almoço**) as such, usually just a coffee, maybe a bread roll. You will see most people have a quick bite in a café just before nipping into work. Lunch (**almoço**) can be a long drawn out affair, usually from 1 – 3 pm, and even in the heat of the summer, the Portuguese eat hot meals in a café. Dinner (**jantar**) is not eaten as late as in Spain, about 8 pm is the norm, and again is a cooked meal. The day's work is interspersed with numerous cups of black coffee. The Portuguese like their food, and large portions are usual in eating places. One thing you can do is ask for **meia-dose** (half-portion), which is quite legitimate. A service charge is not usually included; donate at your discretion, more at dinner than lunch. See Figure 8 for a sample menu and Figure 9 for information on the wines of Portugal.

THE MEDIA

Radio

There is a variety of Portuguese radio channels offering a range of music, discussion and news programmes. The frequencies are listed in all the papers, otherwise simply turn on and try a few out. For English-language programmes try:

◆ RDP (Radio Difusão Portuguesa)
   Lisbon 》 666Khz (mw) 99.4Mhz, 95.7 Mhz (fm)
   Algarve 》 720 Khz (mw) 97.6 Mhz, 88.9 Mhz
   Oporto 》 1377 Khz (mw) 96.7 Mhz

◆ Radio Nova – Wednesdays from 20:00 – 21:00
   Lisbon 》 96.6 Mhz
   Oporto 》 98.9 Mhz

The BBC World service is available at the following frequencies:
   648 Khz / 463 m LW
   9410 Khz / 31 m LW
   12095 Khz / 25 m LW
Reception is variable.

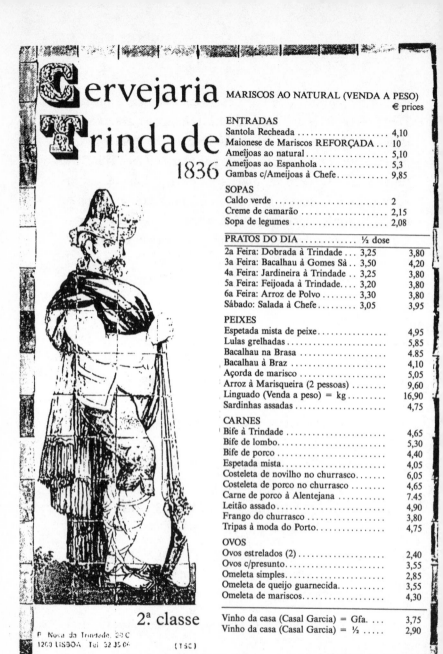

Cervejaria Trindade 1836

2.ª classe

P. Nova da Trindade, 20 C
1200 LISBOA   Tel 32 35 06   (TSC)

MARISCOS AO NATURAL (VENDA A PESO)
€ prices

ENTRADAS
Santola Recheada	4,10
Maionese de Mariscos REFORÇADA	10
Ameïjoas ao natural	5,10
Ameïjoas ao Espanhola	5,3
Gambas c/Ameijoas à Chefe	9,85

SOPAS
Caldo verde	2
Creme de camarão	2,15
Sopa de legumes	2,08

PRATOS DO DIA
		½ dose
2a Feira: Dobrada à Trindade	3,25	3,80
3a Feira: Bacalhau à Gomes Sà	3,50	4,20
4a Feira: Jardineira à Trindade	3,25	3,80
5a Feira: Feijoada à Trindade	3,20	3,80
6a Feira: Arroz de Polvo	3,30	3,80
Sábado: Salada à Chefe	3,05	3,95

PEIXES
Espetada mista de peixe	4,95
Lulas grelhadas	5,85
Bacalhau na Brasa	4.85
Bacalhau à Braz	4,10
Açorda de marisco	5,05
Arroz à Marisqueira (2 pessoas)	9,60
Linguado (Venda a peso) = kg	16,90
Sardinhas assadas	4,75

CARNES
Bife à Trindade	4,65
Bife de lombo	5,30
Bife de porco	4,40
Espetada mista	4,05
Costeleta de novilho no churrasco	6,05
Costeleta de porco no churrasco	4,65
Carne de porco à Alentejana	7.45
Leitão assado	4,90
Frango do churrasco	3,80
Tripas à moda do Porto	4,75

OVOS
Ovos estrelados (2)	2,40
Ovos c/presunto	3,55
Omeleta simples	2,85
Omeleta de queijo guarnecida	3,55
Omeleta de mariscos	4,30

Vinho da casa (Casal Garcia) = Gfa.	3,75
Vinho da casa (Casal Garcia) = ½	2,90

Fig. 8. Sample menu.

Cervejaria Trindade

1836

APERITIVOS E ACEPIPES

	€ prices
Sumo de laranja	2,25
Sumo de tomate	2,25
Porto seco	2,75
Gin tónico	2,70
Cocktail Trindade	3,65

SALGADOS

Croquetes	1,98
Pasteis de bacalhau	1,98
Rissóis de camarão	1,98

DIVERSOS

Manteiga, queijo creme, tartex	1,90
Carnes frias	3,95
Presunto especial	4,05
Melão com presunto	3,55

COMBINADOS

No 1 Prego, presunto e ovo estrelado	3,85
No 2 Carnes frias, salsicha e ovo	3,65
No 3 Pastéis de bacalhau guarnecido	3,00
No 4 Atúm, pão torrado e guarnição	3,90
No 5 Filetes de peixe guarnecidos	3,00

SALADAS

Salada de alface	3,00
Salada de tomate	3,40
Salada mista	2,80
Salada de atúm	4,15

QUEIJOS

Queijo da Serra	3,45
Queijo Flamengo	2,80

FRUTAS

Laranja ou maçã assada	2,50
Melão	2,55
Uvas	2,50
Morangos	2,90

DOCES/SOBREMESAS

Tarte de maçã ou laranja	2,50
Torta de cenoura	2,50
Pudim flan	2,35
Pudim molotov	2,50
Doce de ovos	2,35
Mousse de chocolate	2,55
Gelados vários	3,25
Bolo de amêndoa	2,90

IVA Inc.
Serviço incluido

2ª classe (T.S.C.)

R. Nova do Trindade 20 C
1200 LISBOA Tel 37 35 06

The Red and White Wines of Portugal

In the seventh, and last of our Tesco/ WINE Magazine leaflets, we consider the wines of Portugal, from fresh, crisp Vinho Verde to classic vintage ports.

THE LABEL

ADEGA – winery/cellar.
ANO – year.
BRANCO – white.
CLARETE – light, red table wine.
COLHEITA – vintage.
CRUSTED PORT – a blend of wine from more than one year, with up to four years in cask which makes for earlier drinking. Like vintage port, it throws a sediment or crust.
DOCE – sweet.
ENGARRAFADO POR – bottled by.
ESPUMANTE – sparkling.
GARRAFEIRA – wines usually of an outstanding vintage, which must be aged for two years prior to bottling plus one year in bottle for red wines, and six months ageing prior to bottling and six months in bottle for white wines. There must also be 0.5 degrees of alcohol above the minimum legal alcoholic strength of the wine.
GENEROSO – fortified wine, both dry and sweet.
LBV/LATE-BOTTLED-VINTAGE – a vintage port often from a year in which vintage port is not declared, aged in cask four to six years before bottling. This softens the port so it is ready to drink earlier.
LICOROSO – sweet fortified wine.
MEIO SECO – medium dry.
QUINTA – farm or wine-estate.
REGIÃO DEMARCADA – demarcated wine region.
RESERVA – wine in a year of outstanding quality with the alcoholic strength 0.5 degrees above the minimum legal requirement.
ROSADO – rosé.
RUBY PORT – the cheapest of the red ports – young, blended, sweetly fruity, fortified wine.
SECO – dry.
SINGLE QUINTA PORT – port from a single vineyard, often from a single, undeclared vintage.
TAWNY PORT – fine tawny is racked for a period of years (as stated on the bottle eg 10 years old) while the colour fades and until it stops throwing a deposit. It is a smooth, rich and complex wine, lighter than *vintage port* and less likely to give a hangover. The cheaper style tawny is made by blending red and white ports.

Fig. 9. A guide to Portuguese wines (courtesy of *Tesco's Wine Magazine*)

TINTO – red.
VELHO – old.
VINHO – wine.
VINHO MADURO – any wine intentionally matured for more than one year.
VINHO REGIONAL – similar to the French vins de pays, this is a new
    qualification for superior country wines, to be introduced in 1991.
VINTAGE CHARACTER – inexpensive alternative to vintage port. It is a blend of
    port from more than one year.
VINTAGE PORT – port from a single vintage, it must be bottled within two years
    and then aged. At its best and when fully mature, vintage port is sublime in
    taste.
WHITE PORT – at its best crisp and fresh and ideal as an aperitif. Usually dry,
    there are also a few sweeter versions.

THE REGIONS

ALENTEJO (Ale) A wine region dominated by cooperatives. Until recently the
wines have been very little known outside the area but are now fast gaining
recognition, and are likely to gain *Região Demarcada* status soon.
ALGARVE (Alg) Most famous as a sunny tourist resort, it also produces wine,
mostly red. Its wines received official recognition in 1980 and are adequate, but not
exciting.
BAIRRADA (Bai) A region officially recognised since 1979. The name is derived
from Barro, meaning clay, which is characteristic of the soil. There is an increasing
demand for white and sparkling wines and more white grapes are being planted.
BEIRAS (Bei) An undemarcated region just to the east of *Dão*, divided into Beira
Alta and Beira Baixa, with the most interesting wines coming from the Alta.
BUÇACO (Buc) Lying between the regions of *Bairrada* and *Dão*, the wines made by
the Buçaco Palace Hotel are some of the best reds and white of Portugal.
COLARES (Col) The wine of this region is grown on sand-dunes and consequently
the vines have never been subject to phylloxera like the rest of Europe. The wines
produced are not cheap, but are some of the best traditional-style Portuguese.
DÃO Just west of *Bairrada* is the region of Dão, virtually surrounded by mountains.
The region is best known for its red wines but also produces white.
DOURO (Dou) This area just across the Spanish border is famous for port.
However it does also make an equal amount of table wine, some of which is of high
quality.
ESTREMADURA (Est) Stretching from Lisbon to the Bairrada region, this is
Portugal's largest wine-producing region, with wines which vary from basic, but
pleasant drinking to some exciting, undemarcated wines. *Bucelas, Carcavelos* and
Colares are part of this area but are listed separately.
MADEIRA (Mad) An island off the coast of Morocco whose production of famous
and unique, fortified wine is always being threatened by the more profitable banana.
MINHO (Min) Most famous for its white wine, *Vinho Verde*, there is in fact three
times as much red wine made as white. The region is notable for the vines which
grow in trees or on poles – anything in order to get high above the ground.
RIBATEJO (Rib) This is a large province of mild climate and rich alluvial plans
with the River Tagus winding through.
SETÚBAL (Set) This region gained its official stamp of approval for its sweet,
fortified wines in 1907, but has only recently begun to gain the same recognition for
its table wines.
TRÁS-OS-MONTES (ToM) This is a difficult region for cultivation with its
mountains, thermal springs and river valleys. Mostly red wines are made, and the
producers hope soon to have their own *Região Demarcada*. Also this is an
important source for the country's commercial semi-sweet, semi-sparking rosé.

If you want to listen to some Portuguese radio in the UK, there is a London-based station, VidaNova, broadcasting on MW 558, from 3–4pm on Thursdays.

TV

There are four Portuguese channels broadcasting on the network (RTP1, RTP2, TV1 and SIC). Many programmes, particularly films, are shown in the original language with subtitles in Portuguese. The daily/weekly TV listings are available in both Portuguese and English papers out there and in TV magazines such as *TV Mais*. The Portuguese are very fond of soap operas, particularly Brazilian ones, and a glance through the listings will show you just how many different soaps there are every day.

Cable and satellite are increasingly easy to adopt – ask your neighbours and friends how they had theirs installed. You can also get information from: TV Cabo Tejo SA, Tagus Park, Edif. Inovação II, 414, 2780 Oeiras (Lisbon Area). Tel: 422-7800/ 421-1828.

Newspapers

Portugal has a good range of national journals and magazines, many of a high standard. Regional (local) papers are also usually quite good and may be a starting point if you are trying to extend your Portuguese a bit further. The following papers may be accessed via the Internet – you could have a look right now!

Diário de Notícias	www.dn.pt
Jornal 'O Público'	www.publico.pt
Jornal de Notícias	www.jn.pt
Jornal 'Expresso'	www.expresso.pt

Further website searches can be made using the Altavista search engine. Look for Língua Portuguesa (Portuguese Language) and Jornais (Papers). More useful sites on a variety of themes are listed in Useful Contacts.

English newspapers are widely available in the Algarve, and some kiosks in Lisbon and Oporto. Elsewhere they are more difficult to come by unless you take out a subscription. You will pay a higher cost for the luxury of a paper in English. Useful English publications also on sale in Portugal include the *APN* (*Anglo Portuguese News*), *The News* and *Algarve Resident*.

DOMESTIC SERVICES

Heating

One of the main problems facing many people when entering property in Portugal, and one which is given little thought, is that the houses in general are just not geared up to coping with the winter temperatures. If you arrive in the blistering summer months the last thing on your mind is interior heating – the cool inside your abode is a welcome relief. But be warned: even the Algarve can be cold and wet in the winter, and without central or underfloor heating your time there could be made quite miserable.

It is extremely rare to find central heating in Portuguese property except in the modern apartment and hotel complexes. The summers are long and hot, so heating is not required, therefore why bother installing it for a short time each year? Also, there is very little piped gas supply outside the Lisbon area. It is not unusual in the winter to find people huddled around an electric bar fire, smothered beneath layers of blankets, or more commonly, sitting around a table which houses an electric fire underneath it, hidden beneath the long tablecloth, which is spread onto one's knees. This is less than ideal, so you must consider how you can best heat your property for the colder and invariably damper winter period.

Electric bar fires give out little heat unless you are seated on top of them and as soon as you move away you quickly feel the cold again. Believe me, I've spent a cold, wet Algarvean winter in this way, and a below-freezing December in the Alentejo. Fan heaters give out a wider span of heat, but can be expensive to use. The best and cheapest alternative is to invest in a couple of calor-gas heaters, as these really do boost the heat out, and you can move them from room to room as required. However, they can add moisture to the air and the fumes can make you sleepy. Most houses built now have underfloor or central heating, but make sure the property you invest in is properly insulated.

Electricity
Electricity is 220V with 2-pin round plugs. When you take over new accommodation you should make a note of the meter-reading yourself, then go to the EDP offices (**Electricidade de Portugal**) to inform them of a change of owner/tenant. If you are renting property make sure you know who is responsible for payment of bills, yourself directly or yourself via your landlord. If you are paying direct usually the payments will be debited from a bank account, but until you sort out that side of your affairs (see Chapter 8), you may request to pay cash over the counter. You can also pay via the Multibanco cash machines. You will

receive a monthly bill (**factura/recibo**) which is fairly detailed.

One more point of warning: in the rainy winter period it is common for the electricity supply to be cut off, and frequently so. On one particular day my supply went on and off over seven times. Have plenty of candles ready just in case and watch out if you're writing a book on computer!

Gas

As mentioned earlier, there is little supply of piped gas as yet in Portugal. For heating and cooking purposes when electricity has not been chosen, all requirements are satisfied by calor gas bottles (**garrafa de gás/butano**). These are readily available via specific shops or petrol stations, look for the Gas sign, and delivery can also be arranged. You will have to pay a deposit on the first bottle, if you don't already have one in the property to take back. Then each time you run out the process is simply to return the empty and pay for your next fill. You may need a replacement each month, but this more than anything depends very much on how much cooking you do. Remember also that it will probably be the gas which warms your water supply, so the more hot baths you take, the sooner you should expect to replace the bottle.

Take care when installing the gas bottle and switching on supply, especially if you are not accustomed to them. Ask someone to show you if necessary. The main problem, if any, lies not with the linking up of the bottle to the rubber tube, but the ignition of the pilot light in your boiler, generally located in the kitchen. Usually you will have to press in a button, turn it one way, count a few seconds then slowly let it turn back to its original position. If you have any difficulties, don't worry, most people find them quite fiddly to manoeuvre; simply switch off the supply and go and ask for help. When it is up and running you will find that on opening a hot tap, in the kitchen or bathroom, there will be a roar of flames inside the boiler, as the gas rushes to heat the water, so don't be alarmed. As always with gas, if you smell a suspected leak, switch off the supply and seek help.

Air conditioning

Apart from hotel complexes, and modern villas, most Portuguese buildings do not have an air-conditioning system. In the heat of the summer the shutters are closed on windows, and houses remain in darkness. It's not an ideal system, but for many people it's the best there is.

Water

As with other household services, on taking over tenancy or ownership of a property, let the relevant organisation know there has been a change-over. If you check in your local **câmara** (town hall) they will inform you of what to do; if you are in temporary rented accommodation your landlord will take care of it. Although mains water supplies are becoming more common, it is still quite usual in many places, especially the rural areas, for houses to require their own tank (**cisterna**). This will be filled periodically by a visiting water truck. Having a tank anyway is a good idea in case of drought, when often the water supply is limited or cut off altogether.

Drinking water

As far as drinking tap water is concerned, use your common sense. Although it doesn't do most people any harm it may be prudent to buy bottled water which is very cheap and in the summer months you will need to carry this around with you on any journeys you undertake. The large 5 litre bottles (**garrafão**) usually require a small deposit, and empties returned each time you buy a new one.

Água mineral

| sem gás | flat | fresca | cold |
| com gás | fizzy | natural | room temperature |

Água das pedras is a fizzy water particularly good for stomach upsets and general malaise.

Tap water can be used without trouble for cleaning your teeth, but if you are prone to an upset digestive system you may be better off using a cup of mineral water, especially in the summer when micro-organisms have more chance of survival.

Swimming pools

If you are proud owners of a swimming pool and live in a rural environment, be prepared for your pool water to be used by the emergency services in the common event of forest fires. A helicopter will hover above your pool and let down a tube through which the water is sucked up. Just let them get on with it, the alternative is complete devastation of the countryside.

COMMUNICATIONS

Private phones

Many a horror story has been told by both ex-pats and

Portuguese nationals alike of the frustratingly long process involved in having one's own phone installed, be it at home or in your business. Even after registering, delays of up to 2 and 3 years before actual installation have been known, without any apologies or apparent reason, although it may be said that should you choose to live 6 miles up a beaten track in the middle of nowhere, perhaps you could be expected to wait for the phone lines to catch up with you! However, the good news by all accounts is that delays are shortening and recent reports in some areas suggest the wait can be a matter of a few weeks. If you have any connections where you are staying it pays to speak to them first, as I was promised a phone within three weeks, providing I had the necessary documents, thanks to my contact with one of the influential senhoras of the town.

How to apply for a phone
You will need the following documents:

- residência
- ID – passport will do
- card with tax number (**carta de contribuinte**)
- proof of where you live
- possibly proof of bank account.

If you take these to the local Telecom office (**Loja da Telecom**) they will inform you of possible delays, and supply you with a list of prices (**tabela de preços**). You should expect to pay an installation fee and a monthly rental in addition to the cost of your calls.

Call charges
Most calls fall into the following categories:

+ local call
+ regional (up to 50km)
+ national (over 50km)
+ Europe

Tariffs are available from the Telecom shop.

If you want to make a reverse call you will ask for **uma chamada a pagar no destino**, and will be asked for your number, the name of the person to receive the call and their number. Cheaper rates are available after 9 pm. Services such as 'friends and family', voice mail and itemised billing are now widely available.

Public phones
Once you have deciphered how to open the folding doors on the booth, you are faced with a phone with a long slot on the top of it. Instructions in Portuguese, English and French are normally on display, along with a pictorial guide, but as a rule, follow these basic steps:

+ put a selection of coins (**moedas**) into the slot alongside each other, with the minimum required ready to drop down first. Alternatively, insert a phone card (**credifone**) in the appropriate slot.

+ pick up the receiver and listen for the tone

+ dial your number, along with any necessary codes as below

- you should hear a dialling tone, longish and intermittent

- the first coin will drop down when the line is connected and the remaining coins will follow suit as required, if it's working properly.

Main town telephone codes

Albufeira	289	Aveiro	234	Beja	284
Braga	253	Cascais	21	Coimbra	239
Elvas	268	Estoril	21	Evora	266
Faro	289	Lagos	282	Lisboa	21
Loulé	289	Portimão	282	Porto	22
Setubal	265	Tavira	281	Tomar	249

To dial from the UK, the code is 00-351-local code-number. From Portugal to the UK dial 00-44-code (minus 0)-number.

If you have family in the UK who may ring you frequently in Portugal, it's worth contacting 'One.Tel' phone company, on 020 7331 977, who offer cheap services abroad.

Mobile phones

These are becoming more widely used in Portugal, particularly by the business community. If you already own a mobile phone check with your network to see if it will pick up and transmit in Portugal. Otherwise, once there you can get information from:

Telecel, Comunicações Pessoais, Rua Tomás Fonseca, Torre A 13, 1600 Lisboa. Tel: 21-7272001.
TMN, Telecomunicações Móveis Nacionais, Avenida 5 de Outubro, 208, 1050 Lisboa. Tel: 21-7914400.
Optimus, Avenida dos Combatentes No 43, Edifício

Green Park 13, 1600 Lisboa. Tel: 21-7233600.

You may also find phone shops local to where you are living. Whilst driving only hands-free phone systems may be used.

Walkie-talkies – portable radio telephonic transmitting/receiving sets are not permitted.

If you have a CB, temporary licences for 30 days' use can be obtained from the Instituto das Comunicações de Portugal (ICP), Av. José Malhoa No 12, 1070 Lisboa. Tel: 21-7211000. Internet: www.icp.pt

POSTAL SERVICES

Most post offices (**correios**) open from 9 am to 6 pm, with a lunchtime break from 12.30 pm to 2.30 pm. A larger service is easier to find in the bigger cities such as Lisbon or Oporto, where you will discover a more extensive network of branches. However, apart from the more remote villages out in the countryside, most towns do have their own office. You can make use of the Correios for all your postal requirements, but be forewarned, a lot of patience and a sense of humour come in handy when you are six or seven back in a queue and the assistant has decided to have a chat with her colleague. This is an all too regular occurrence in the more provincial branches and it can take a little getting used to, especially if you are the efficient type. I was so frustrated one day in my local branch I almost volunteered to get behind the counter and help out. Apart from the delay, proceedings usually go smoothly.

How to use the service

- Sending a letter (**enviar uma carta**). Internal mail costs approx 30 cents, and to the EU 50 cents. Once you have bought your stamps you may need to look for the mail box (**caixa**) which is usually on the wall outside. Alternatively your letter may be franked by the clerk and unceremoniously flung into a waiting box.

- Sending a parcel (**um pacote**). A similar procedure to that above, but you may have to pop the parcel onto the scales (**balança**), and fill in a customs declaration slip.

- Picking up mail. If you have decided to have your mail kept at the correios in a box (**apartado**), you will either be allocated a small box and issued with a key, or will have to ask for your mail over the counter. An apartado is useful if you live somewhere quite rural with less frequent deliveries, or if your property has a less than convenient mail system. The apartado is easy to apply for, simply fill in another form.

- Sending valuable items. You can either ask to send this **registrado**, or use the system of **valores declarados**, where you declare the value, in euros, on the outside of the packet, up to 2kg in weight allowed. A small insurance levy is made, and any loss or damage will be indemnified.

- Making a phone call. Many post offices have 2 or 3 telephone cabins (**cabines**). You must ask at the desk to make a call (**fazer uma chamada**), and you will be allocated a cabin. When you have finished the call, pay at the counter. Calls made this way are far costlier than tackling a public phone booth. See previous section on public phones.

Electronic communication

Fax

Fax machines are widely used throughout the country. Some small businesses offer a fax service – look around for signs in shop windows, either those offering administrative/secretarial services, or even estate agents, bookshops or hotels may be able to help should you need to send or receive a fax.

Internet and email

The Internet has reached most corners of the globe and Portugal is no exception. Apart from the smaller villages and rural locations, many people by now have access to the Web. If you have your own PC and connection, check with your provider whether the service is still valid in Portugal. There are some service providers now operating in Portugal, including Telepac (Portugal Telecom), which may prove to be a cheaper option than continuing with your own provider. Useful email and Internet addresses are included in the Contacts section on page 176.

CHECKLIST

1. Have you registered at the Consulate and applied for Residency if appropriate?
2. Are you familiar with the currency and its relative value?
3. How far are you going to integrate into the society and learn the language?
4. Have you tried out local shopping and cuisine?
5. Have you made arrangements to pay for your utilities?
6. Do you need to make special provision for service supply to a mobile phone or Internet?

Working in Portugal

WORK PERMITS

Members of EU countries do not need a work permit to take up employment in Portugal, and do not need to register with the Ministry of Labour. You will be treated on a par with Portuguese nationals. However, you do need to adhere to the regulations governing Residency, and you require a formal work contract on the same basis as for Portuguese workers.

Another thing to bear in mind is that, despite the lifting of employment restrictions and the theoretical policy that any EU national can take up work wherever they wish, the application procedure for any job will be as it is in one's own country, and within some companies preference may still be given to Portuguese nationals. You will always stand a much better chance of work if you have at least a working knowledge of the language.

LOOKING FOR WORK

Your search for employment may begin in the UK, by scouring papers such as the *Times Educational Supplement*, the *Guardian Education* section, for teaching positions, or by contacting organisations dealing solely with jobs abroad, again often advertised in journals. If, on the other hand, you have already landed in Portugal and have decided to try your luck, the following suggestions may help your search:

♦ English periodicals such as *The News*, *APN*, *Algarve Resident*, wherein you will find a selection of jobs from teaching to secretarial, to advertising and sales.

♦ Portuguese journals such as *Diário de Notícias*, *Correio da Manhã*; of course the majority of these jobs will be for Portuguese companies, with some multinationals or language schools also advertising.

♦ Job agencies, especially in the larger cities you may find English-run agencies, such as Manpower in Lisbon, who act just as they would in the UK, so it's a good idea to have copies of CVs and references, and make a personal contact if possible. More than anything they will have an abundance of secretarial work. You will also find smaller agencies locally in the Algarve.

♦ On spec enquiries – you can try hawking your wares, by writing on spec to hotels/businesses/organisations, asking about potential work; try to follow this up with a meeting with the manager (**gerente**) or (**director/a**), as often letters tend to be pushed aside initially.

♦ Asking around – be prepared to use up a bit of shoe leather and have the nerve to ask on the spot for work. This can often be effective with manual labour. Use any contacts you have and get them to ask around for you as well.

♦ Place ads yourself – in papers, bar noticeboards, in shops and so on.

UK OR PORTUGUESE COMPANY?

With the advent of EU regulations concerning non-nationals working, the range of jobs has widened significantly. Before, the strict laws on work permits and tax problems meant that choice was rather limited, and often involved an element of illegal movement. Now non-nationals have the same rights as Portuguese nationals to employment, as is the general case throughout the EU member states. However, this doesn't mean to say you should expect to walk into any job you like, and without any knowledge of the language, you will have difficulty.

UK companies

Maybe working for a company whose name you recognise would make you feel more secure, and indeed, you may have been sent out from the UK to take up a position within a Portuguese branch of your own employer. Whichever, it seems comforting to be within the clutches of a household name. You will find however, that most of the Portugal-based branches are run by a management team of Portuguese nationals, most of the work is conducted in their language, and you soon have to learn it to fit in adequately.

Portuguese companies

They could be liable to have more bias towards their own nationals when offering work, although now there should be an equal opportunity, that of the best man/woman. You may be considered an asset, being a native-English speaker, but again it cannot be emphasised enough that with little knowledge of their language, your choice of job will still remain very limited.

CURRICULUM VITAE

DADOS PESSOAIS
Nome: Jane Smith
Data de nascimento: 29 de Outubro de 1970
Estado Civil: Solteira
Morada: Rua das Flores, 3 – 4151- 213 Porto
Telefone: 22-4677823

HABILITAÇÕES LITERÁRIAS:
1989/1993 –   Curso superior B.A. de Estudos Europeus e Economia na Universidade de Londres (Goldsmiths College). Concluído com a classificação 2:1.

CONHECIMENTOS DE LÍNGUA ESTRANGEIRAS:

	FALADO	LIDO	ESCRITO
INGLÊS (Língua materna)	bom	bom	bom
PORTUGUÊS	bom	bom	bom
ESPANHOL	bom	bom	bom
FRANCÊS	médio	regular	fraco

OUTRAS HABILITAÇÕES:
1995 – Curso de Informática ao nível do utilizador na escola Centre for Computer Studies, em Londres.
1997 – Curso de Relações Públicas, no Institute of Business Studies, em Birmingham, Inglaterra.

EXPERIÊNCIA PROFISSIONAL:
1993/1995 – Secretária do gerente da agência de viagens World Tours Ltd., de Londres.
1995/1997 – Coordenadora do balcão da mesma Agência em Birmingham. Responsável pelo recrutamento de pessoal e lançamento dos programas da Agência.
1997/1999 – Chefe da secção de exportação do armazém Debenhams, em Londres.

OUTRAS INFORMAÇÕES:
Possuidora de carta de condução
Actualmente residente em Portugal, a frequentar o curso de Marketing, na Universidade do Porto e exercendo, de vez em quando, as funções de tradutora e intérprete em várias empresas britânicas.

Fig. 10. Sample of a CV in Portuguese.

Porto, 20 de Maio de 200X

Exmos. Senhores:
   Li no Jornal de Notícias de 20 de Maio que pretendem admitir uma colaboradora para a área administrativa da empresa de V.Exas.
   Creio que reúno os requisitos descritos no anúncio e a vaga anunciada vem de encontro às minhas ambições e interesses. Como terão oportunidade de observar através do Currículum Vitae em anexo, a minha experiência profissional será vantajosa para a empresa.

Com os melhores cumprimentos

Atenciosamente

Jane Smith

Fig. 11. Sample of a job application letter.

TEACHING

If you intend to stay long term in Portugal, then the chances of your finding teaching work are considerably better than for fleeting visitors looking for a few euros to 'tide them over'. Obviously, very much depends on the subject you offer and your qualifications and experience; however, you will always find some establishments willing to take on non-qualified teachers, especially for EFL (English as a foreign language).

Teaching English as a foreign language (TEFL)
The number of English language schools is on the increase and a scan through the *Yellow Pages* under Escolas/Institutos de Línguas, will give you a lead to follow up. Most are Portuguese-run, despite their very English names, such as Oxford/Cambridge school, and usually the best approach is the direct one. Try and have copies of CVs/

diplomas with you and try visiting a few places enquiring for possible work. You will often be told of coming work or may arrange an interview, and you can leave your details with a relevant person. Alternatively, a letter-run to a dozen or so schools may set the ball rolling, but don't expect instant replies. Many schools take on non-diploma holders if they are short-staffed, and your general appearance and attitude appears positive. TEFL work is always advertised in all the English daily and weekend papers, and can be arranged before you leave the UK. Two excellent publications are: the *EL Gazette*, published monthly and listing world-wide vacancies, and the *ELT Guide* published annually. Tel: (020) 7255 1969.

If you have no luck with official teaching, an ad in the local paper/school noticeboard/corner shops, advertising private lessons will usually come up with some work. I once hit a town with small hand-outs printed on a word processor, even sticking them inside telephone kiosks, which provided interest. But do be careful where you place them; ask permission if applicable. If you can, ask around for the going rate, but be prepared to charge less than UK prices if you want to secure some pupils. For a comprehensive guide to teaching English, check out *Teach English as a Foreign Language* (How To Books).

Other subjects
This work is harder to come by. Up until recently, non-nationals could not work in a state school, and even visiting lecturers sometimes found it difficult to cut through the tremendous red tape. Now with the EU changes, things are set to be different. However, don't count on a job in the Portu-

guese system as a foregone conclusion, as the process to be accepted will still take time. Your best bet if you are a teacher looking for work is to try your luck at some of the International schools, both British and American. A comprehensive list of these is included in Chapter 10 on education and in Useful Contacts, and further details can be obtained from the British Council.

If you can, write to the schools before you go to Portugal explaining your background and your interest in their school. You will find that it's then easier to arrange an interview on arrival if the school has had time to digest your material. As most schools strictly follow a recognised curriculum it can be difficult to arrange work if you are not qualified; however, they may need stand-in teachers for a while, and some schools are venturing into evening classes for parents which would provide you with an opening. Yet these still have to prove their viability, especially on the Algarve, where the emphasis outside school is very much a non-educational one.

Do be cautious, though, in accepting work from schools without checking out their own background. A read through the warnings at the end of this chapter and that on education will show you that things can go disastrously wrong if you make a bad choice.

FREELANCE OPPORTUNITIES

If you don't want to be tied to a particular job or location, doing freelance work may be an attractive option; however, all will depend very much on your field of work and skills.

Journalism

As a journalist/writer/photographer you can try hawking your services round the English-language publications, many of which are situated in the Algarve. The likes of papers such as *The News/APN/Algarve Resident*, and glossy magazines such as *Algarve Gazette* and the *Algarve Magazine* are all open to suggestions, but you may find the same old names appearing across the board, and authors jealously guarding their patch. The quality of journalism is often not very high, so don't expect to use it as a stepping stone into the cut-throat world of reporting. Pay averages about £50–60 per 1000 words. If you speak the lingo and have a small portfolio with you, you could try the Portuguese publications, but again, competition is tough.

Other possibilities

People have set themselves up as:

- sign-writers/poster designers/golf-club artists
- computer consultants/IT support
- translators/interpreters
- typists
- home-helps/handypersons
- sports instructors.

In fact, if you have a car and with a bit of publicity, there is no end to the choices. For details of your tax position as a self-employed person see the next chapter.

JOBS IN AGRICULTURE

Portugal isn't one of the European countries that people immediately head for with the idea of fruit-picking or harvesting as a means of working their stay there. In most books on European agricultural work Portugal is conspicuous by its absence. This is probably due to the fact that although a great deal of land is agricultural, the communities who work that land involve everybody available, so not much opportunity arises for outsiders. On top of this, farming people have little enough money to spend on their families let alone to hire itinerant workers. The farming situation is very difficult at the moment, and many farms are left abandoned, their owners departed to try and find a living elsewhere.

In the wealthier, wine growing districts of Northern Portugal, the Minho/Douro areas, you may find some work picking grapes. The grape harvest or **vindímia**, takes place in the autumn. You could try writing first to some of the well-known port wine companies, asking for assistance or try approaching some of the larger quintas (estates) and enquiring. Pay will be minimal, but you will always be given shelter and food. Work is laboriously hard, so you should be fit and hardy. The rewards in companionship are great as the Portuguese work hard but also know how to relax afterwards.

Other people have successfully answered ads placed by expats in publications such as *Organic Gardening* journals and newsletters, asking for help.

The land (**a terra**) is vitally important to the Portuguese and working on it should bring you closer in contact with their true character.

VOLUNTEER WORK

An alternative way to work on the land if that is what you really enjoy. Work camps may be short (2–3 weeks) or up to 6 months, and you will most likely need to pay your own transport and pocket money, but food and lodgings are provided. Try the following organisations.

◆ Central Bureau for exchange visits.

◆ UK agricultural colleges, some have Portugal-UK exchanges and may be able to help.

◆ ATEJ Associação de Turismo Estudantil e Juvenil, R. Miguel Bombarda 425, 4000 Oporto.

◆ Companheiros Construtores, R. Pedro Monteiro, 3-1°, Coimbra.

◆ FAOJ Fundo de Apoio aos Organismos Juvenis, R. Duque de Avila 137, 1097 Lisboa Codex.

◆ Turicoop, R. Pascoal de Melo 15-1° Dto., 1100 Lisboa.

CASUAL/PART- OR FULL-TIME WORK

The kind of employment you look for will no doubt depend on the following factors:

◆ how long you intend to stay there
◆ where you intend to stay
◆ what your skills/expertise are
◆ if you have a family to support
◆ your outgoing payments for accommodation/food/ bills.

Casual

This type of work is ideal for anyone with no firm plans as

to their time/location. It isn't too easy to come across, and usually involves a lot of asking around, and often pay may be in the form of food or accommodation. The places to ask are restaurants for kitchen work, hotels for general portering, large villas for cleaning and handy jobs or pool cleaning, larger stores and holiday complexes. You may be able to get leaflet distribution work.

You are more likely to find this kind of work in the tourist regions, but you might just be able to work your way around the whole country, but do expect difficulties in the remote country regions (although no Portuguese would turn a hungry visitor away from their door).

Part-time

Students, housewives, or anyone needing a little extra may find work in supermarkets, teaching, setting up children-watch groups, restaurants, or offices (reception/secretarial). Some help can be found from the few job agencies, but again, asking around is essential and unless you have a command of the language you will be mainly restricted to the holiday spots.

Full-time

If you haven't already arrived in Portugal by means of a company relocation but are seeking a permanent job, your procedure will be as that at home – employment agencies, direct contact with companies, asking around, and selling your skills in a market-place of equally eager potential employees. Working full time involves a different working day, correct business etiquette and complete declaration of earnings and deductions, so be aware of the system (see tax section).

YOUR CONTRACT OF EMPLOYMENT

With any kind of paid work (unless you are paid cash in hand or with food in return for help), you must make sure you have a legal contract and understand the implications of its contents. The main sections you should verify before signing a contract and undertaking the job should include the following:

◆ **Temporary suspension of contract** – Portuguese law allows contracts to be suspended in the case of unexpected situations, out of the company's hands, which affect the normal running of business (eg, natural disasters).

◆ **Termination of contract** – the usual reasons you would expect (retirement/mutual agreement/just dismissal/collective dismissal). Be aware, also, that if market forces lead the company into an unviable position the company may decide a certain job must cease to exist.

◆ **Term of employment** – in some circumstances, the law allows short-term periods of work to be written into a contract (known as a limited-term contract), especially when employees are in their first job. You should check if this applies to you. If your contract is for a fixed term which is subject to renewal, be aware that it can only be renewed twice, and its maximum length of duration not more than three years. Otherwise, if you are lucky enough to be offered an indeterminate period, usually long term, ensure that everything is officially down in writing and signed by both parties. Remember that a document is worth nothing without the signature of both parties. Both indefinite and limited-term contract work is subject to a trial period which must also be specified in writing.

◆ **Working hours** – average 35–44 hours per week. Usually one day off per week, but many companies adopt a five-day week policy. The maximum legal working day is eight hours.

◆ **Holidays** – 22 working days annually.

◆ **Wages** – the legal minimum salary is approx. £200 per month. Salaries are fixed as monthly amounts and usually paid monthly. Employees usually receive 14 salary payments a year, with the extra payments at Christmas and as a holiday subsidy.

TAX LIABILITY

As well as your contract you should thoroughly check and understand the Portuguese tax system and your contribution to it.

IRS (personal income tax)

Payable by all residents and non-residents. If you are a resident, ie. if you spend 183 days or more per calendar year in Portugal, or if you have residential accommodation which would suggest it is an habitual residence, that is that you frequently inhabit it, you will be taxed on total income from inside and outside Portuguese territory. Non-residents are only taxed on income received inside Portugal (see also pp. 49–50). There are tax bands from 15 to 40% and categories included such as interest on bank accounts, shares and royalties. Allowances include: health and education expenses (very useful as prices here are high), payments to retirement homes, and insurance premiums, amongst others.

How to register

♦ Take a copy of your contract to your local **Finanças** to be registered, unless your company undertakes to do this for you.

♦ Your residency documents, issued by the **Serviço de Estrangeiros**, will give you a social security number (**número de contribuinte**), which should also be indicated to the Finanças.

♦ You will be sent tax returns forms to complete at the end of each tax year.

INSURANCE

National Insurance (NI) – Caixa

Your employer should register you but it is up to you to check this has been done. Monthly contributions, calculated on gross salary are approximately: employer 24% and employee 11%. This contribution will cover you, as in the UK, for entitlement to treatment in the health system. Many companies also offer a separate scheme. If you are only working temporarily, and contribute to a compulsory scheme in the UK, you will be exempt from payments under the 'relief from double social security' scheme.

Independant insurance

This is entirely your own choice. Some companies offer

incentives such as payment towards this themselves. The Portuguese health system has often been criticised, so you must work out the pros and cons, and decide how much extra you can afford, and what risks are involved.

A report published by the Portuguese National Statistics Institute in May 2002 revealed that the Portuguese system of taxation is out-dated and out of line with many other fiscal systems in Europe. It remains to be seen, however, what changes will result from the findings, and how long they will take to implement. Employing a reputable accountant (**contabilista**), or seeking advice from tax consultants is prudent if you have any doubts.

STATE BENEFITS

Unemployment benefits

Anyone who has received this benefit for over four weeks in the UK can have the same benefit (UK rate) paid for up to three months, whilst looking for work in the EU. You must advise your own DSS office a good while before you depart, and you will be issued with **form E303**, to hand in to the Portuguese employment authorities (**Ministério de Emprego e Segurança Social**). Be prepared for delays, but as long as the relevant documentation is accompanying you, you should experience no problems in receiving benefit. You can also claim unemployment benefit from the Portuguese state, if you have worked there and paid contributions into the caixa fund (any contribution you have made in other EU countries can also count). As in the UK, various criteria apply in order for you to become eligible for benefit. Contact the local **Centro de Emprego** or **Centro Regional de Segurança Social**. The unemployment rate in Portugal rose slightly in 2001, to a current 4.4%. The highest number of unemployed is in the Alentejo region, the lowest on the island of Madeira.

You can also receive your state pension once in Portugal, and any work done in other EU member states will count towards it (see Chapter 7).

Useful publications by the DSS

Leaflet SA29 — *Your social security, health care and pension rights in the European Community.*
Social security for migrant workers (now a little outdated).
Leaflet UBL22 – *Unemployment benefit for people going abroad.*
Leaflet N138 – *Social Security abroad.*
Working in Portugal by the Employment Service.

Contact: Overseas branch DSS, Newcastle upon Tyne NE98 1YX, or your local DSS/Job centre.

BE CAREFUL!

Although work permits are now no longer necessary, allowing the foreign visitor to Portugal one less document to worry about, it can nevertheless be easy to get carried away by the seemingly casual lifestyle and amicable business methods. Don't forget to check that you are properly registered for tax and NI and that your contract is completely in order. Potentially, your situation is highly jeopardised should authorities decide to check your company's documents and find things amiss. I have heard of employers who deducted caixa contributions from their employees' wages yet because they had not even registered them as employees in the first place (and therefore they did not possess a número de contribuinte), that money was obviously not winging its way to the Finanças office. The same employer worded his contract in such a way that the employees had no rights whatsoever regarding length of employment and the contract could be terminated without just cause. As the contracts are in Portuguese, it certainly pays to understand the language or at least have someone check things over for you first.

Don't assume that working for an English firm gives you any added security. The employer mentioned above was English – I know because I worked for him for a while under those conditions. The Algarve particularly is full of ex-pats who for one reason or another (some more dubious than others) have decided to make a living through bars/shops/schools/property. Often their business is here one day and gone the next – so do check out potential employers' backgrounds as much as you can.

CHECKLIST
1. Have you drawn up an action plan and a list of contacts for finding work?
2. Do you have copies of all relevant certificates, diplomas and CVs?
3. Have you thought about your skills and decided what type of work you want?
4. Have you fully checked, and do you understand, your contract of employment?
5. Have you registered for caixa payments and do you have your número de contribuinte?
6. Do you have all the necessary unemployment documentation?

Setting Up in Business

WHICH REGION?

The location of your business will depend on certain factors such as:

- what type of business is intended
- what area is most suited to that
- can that area stand more competition
- where would you be happy living.

You are going to have to do your homework and plan your project well in order to get financial backing, and the region you decide on will play a large part in your business's success or failure. Among the areas you should consider are:

- **Around Oporto** – traditionally the home of the great port wine industry and historically linked with English commerce, Oporto itself is a busy thriving city with good communication links. Surrounded by lush countryside, and not far from popular coastal resorts, there is something for everyone.

- **Lisbon and District** – the cosmopolitan capital, home to many international companies and financial institutions, a truly business-like city, ideally placed for domestic and international travel. Scope for tourist-style business around the coastline, in places such as Cascais and Estoril.

◆ **Setúbal** – south of river from Lisbon, heavily industrialised, and now developed to accommodate a new Ford/VW factory. New infrastructure is bringing a good range of services.

◆ **Algarve** – almost totally geared up to tourist trade, all year round. Leisure amenities, hotel trade, food and drink, and related services.

The region you choose will also dictate the price of any property you may require, so that also needs to be taken into consideration. Office/floor space in Lisbon and Oporto is at a premium, either to purchase or rent, but elsewhere you should be able to find suitable premises, depending on your intentions.

For science and technology businesses, you may benefit from the shared service centres at:

Taguspark, Rua Comandante Cordeiro Castanheira, 41, 2° esq. 2780 Oeiras. Contact Mr Vasco Varela.
Associação para o Parque de Ciência e Tecnologia, Av. da Boavista, 1245, 4° esq. 4100 Porto. Contact Mrs Candida Loureiro.

OPPORTUNITIES AVAILABLE

How big are you thinking? If your plans are rather grand, and include maybe setting up some kind of export trade between Portugal/UK, your first step should be to contact the Portuguese-UK Chamber of Commerce, whose members on both sides of the Atlantic come from a wide range of industry and commerce and the Chamber offers useful advice, contacts and promotional events. Their publications also give full details of doing business with Portugal. Contact Mr Ronnie Price, Portuguese-UK Chamber of Commerce, 4th Floor, 22/25a Sackville Street, London W1X 1DE. Tel: (020) 7494 1844. Email: admin@pukc.demon.co.uk

On a smaller scale, what other opportunities are open to you? At the moment Portugal still lacks a full workforce competent to deal with the latest technology, so any kind of computer-related work and training will be welcomed. Grant aid is available, especially for this kind of initiative (information from the Portuguese Foreign Investment Institute, see Useful Contacts). In the tourist areas your initial scope is perhaps wider, despite a plentiful supply of various existing services. After all, there are a lot of tourists to go round! Bars, pubs, eating places, boutiques, guest-houses, leisure activities, beauty treatment, you name it, the tourist will indulge in it. But there are also the locals to consider – they depend on services all year round, so you have an even wider market.

One thing to bear in mind is that in places like the Algarve there is a growing feeling that the tourist boom has outstayed its welcome to some extent, and that new (and existing) business should be geared more towards 'quality' tourism. A large house in a country setting could be home to cultural activities, such as painting and literary holidays; special care should be taken to ensure the countryside is left intact and that property is in keeping with cultural and natural tradition.

Your best bet is always to have an exploratory trip to weigh up the possibilities, before spending money and effort on what might turn out to be a white elephant.

Further guidance can be obtained from: DTI – Portugal desk.

CASE HISTORIES

Jeep tours

A pair of enterprising ex-pats formed a partnership and created an adventure company called Jumbo Jeep Tours. After many months of researching the history, culture, and natural life of the Algarve, and having journeyed extensively into unknown areas inland from the more tourist-laden coastline, mapping out interesting off-beat routes, the pair pooled their resources and invested in two brand new tough jeeps. With the right publicity, they found they had a market for these unusual trips. The jeeps had a couple of itineraries – all day or half day trips into the hills, or evening rides out with a lavish Portuguese dinner at a local wine cellar. Having been on two such journeys to review the service for a travel article, I can vouch for the fact that the partners had certainly done their homework – the journeys were very informative and thoroughly entertaining.

Problems experienced

Some of the main problems they came up against were:

♦ Initially, no rural maps available – only the army has access to these – therefore necessitated a lot of investigation of tracks and routes on their own.

- Often police road checks involved lengthy discussion as to ownership of the jeep, especially relating to how many passengers it was allowed to carry (and having relevant insurance documents).

- Publicity/promotion – always a problem, at first, knowing how much to spend. Leaflets around holiday complexes helped, as did articles such as mine in the glossy magazines.

- The weather – summer forest fires which devastated Monchique deprived them of a route for some time. Heat conditions always had to be monitored.

House/pet sitting

Mrs Jean Spencer found herself faced with the dilemma, half through necessity, half by choice, of either returning to the UK to continue her life or to stay in Portugal with friends she had made, and eke out a living for herself. On her own for the first time in many years, the choice was not an easy one, but the determined lady decided to stay in the countryside she had come to love, with the pressure-free lifestyle she now appreciated, and turned her mind to supporting herself. Without a good knowledge of the language her possibilities could only lie within the ex-pat community.

Living in a rural area, Jean knew only too well the problems facing ex-pats wanting to visit their home country for a while, but afraid to leave their villas prey to gangs of thieves who seem to know exactly which ex-pat villa to attack at what time. The other problem was what to do with family pets. So Jean came up with the idea of pet/

villa sitting. Jean either welcomed pets in her own home for a while, or alternatively, she relocated to an owner's villa, keeping a watchful eye on both property and pets, leaving relieved owners to travel abroad safely without the fear of a tragic return. Jean began by spreading the word to friends, and immediately took over the care of someone's dog for a fortnight. From there, with the help of a bit of publicity, some business cards and leaflets, Jean happily made a living for herself. The initial idea was very simple, but in the end proved a winner.

Art and design

Neil Johnson and his wife had visited Portugal on many occasions and decided to take the plunge and relocate there. Neil, as a professional designer and a talented artist, was sure he could find something in his line of work to support them.

Initially Neil painted local scenes and sold them through various outlets. He then had the enterprising idea to contact golf clubs and offer his services as a sort of 'artist in semi-residence' to them. Members could purchase paintings of various holes on the course, either with or without their own presence in the picture; an ideal souvenir, especially attractive to businesses entertaining corporate clients. Neil also won a contract to paint a mural at one club, and other jobs started to come his way. His reputation as a quality artist soon spread and he was invited to provide the artist's impressions of the new Vasco da Gama bridge in Lisbon.

Neil then bumped into Una Maddison, a long-time

resident in the Algarve and another talented artist. Together they have set up joint exhibitions of their work, and Una, along with husband Peter (retired headmaster of the International School in Porches) and son Brendan, were inspired to set up an art school at their villa in Lagos. The Camilo Artes Studio offers drawing and painting classes in various techniques, including pastels, oils and fabric design. They have daily and weekly courses, or visitors can drop in on an ad-hoc basis. You can contact Una (and through her gain access to the art scene in the Algarve) at: Casa Tenente Camilo, Praia do Porto de Mós, 8600 Lagos, Algarve. Tel: (351)-282-760129.

HOW TO FORM A COMPANY

Whether you are to be a sole trader/partnership/or company with a number of employees, the basic steps for application for approval and registration of your intent and all other subsequent stages of the process are similar. Differences occur depending on the type of business structure you intend, mainly:

- Sole trader with unlimited liability or limited liability – **estabelecimento individual de responsabilidade limitada (RIRL)**
- General partnership – **sociedade em nome colectiva (SNC)**
- Private limited liability company – **sociedade por quotas (Lda)**
- Corporation – **sociedade anónima (SA)**

You should seek legal and financial guidance before you embark upon any one route, and the timescale shown in

Figure 12 should give you an idea of what is involved in setting up. Seek information from the Instituto do Investimento Estrangeiro (Foreign Investment Institute), Av. da Liberdade, 258-4°, 1200 Lisboa. Three useful publications are:

- *Doing Business in Portugal*, Price Waterhouse.
- *Guide to Investing in Portugal*, Arthur Andersen & Co.
- *Doing Business in Portugal*, Ernst & Young.

TAX/NI/VAT

You must check very carefully your position for tax and contributions, as it is all too easy to get lost (deliberately or not) in the maze of administration. But with the assistance of a reliable financier/accountant you should not have too much to worry about.

WEEKS	1	2	3	4	5	6	7	8	9	10	11	12	13	14	15	16
Approval of name	*															
Deposit of capital with credit institution			*													
Public deed of incorporation					*	*										
Registration as a taxpayer						*										
Commercial registry and national registry of collective persons						*	*	*	*	*						
Stamping of company books											*	*	*	*		
Publication in official gazette													*	*	*	*

From: Practical Aspects of Estabishing a Business in Portugal – ICEP/Arthur Andersen

Fig. 12. Typical timescale for setting up a Portuguese company (times may vary from case to case).

If you have formed a company you will be expected to keep accounts, to be audited annually, and your corporate income tax (**imposto sobre o rendimento das pessoas colectivas, IRC**) is made via three payments during the following year. The difference between what has been paid and that actually due is made up when the income tax returns have been submitted (31 May of the following year). Your taxable profits are worked out in very much the same way as they would be in UK, with certain provisions made in the calculations. A useful publication explaining this in detail is the *Guide to Investing in Portugal* by Banco Totta and Açores/Arthur Andersen. Don't forget that as a company you are also liable for payment of the employees' contribution to the **caixa** (NI).

For self-employed as for ordinary employees, your tax is the individual income tax (IRS mentioned in the previous chapter). However, many business expenses can be deducted before your profit is calculated. These may include: health expenses/education/compulsory pension payments. There are also personal allowances. As self-employed you are also liable for caixa contributions, but again there are a number of exemptions such as travel expenses and canteen subsidies.

Whatever your business status, check also your position for VAT (IVA, **Imposto sobre o valor acrescentado**), as for stages of production/wholesale/retail, VAT can be offset against what you may have paid on your own supplies. Happily, in 2001, Portugal recorded the lowest number of insolvencies in Europe; with some wise planning your business stands a chance of success.

BUSINESS ETIQUETTE

Dress

One of the first things to strike you about Portuguese people going about their business, be it in a bank, office or hotel, is how smartly dressed they are. I once had the opportunity to sit for a couple of hours at a Lisbon café, having arrived extremely early in the morning, too early in fact to book into my guest house. As Lisbon came alive and the bustle of the capital city began, I was very impressed by the immaculate appearance of the passers-by. You don't necessarily have to don pinstripe and bowler hat, but ties and jackets are the norm, with casual but smart suits or dresses for the ladies. If you want to be taken seriously in your venture, think about how the Portuguese will first see you.

Appointments

The Portuguese are notoriously difficult to tie down to specific times and if you need to make an appointment to see someone, unless you have been personally introduced you should try approaching by letter, but be prepared to follow this up with a phone call (at least one), and be persistent until you have arranged a date.

As far as appointments and meetings are concerned, you will have to exert a tremendous amount of staying power and patience, as it is extremely common to be kept waiting, sometimes as long as an hour or two, before your appointment is kept. This is awfully frustrating, but should you opt either to arrive late yourself, or to blow your top, you will find great difficulty rearranging a new meeting. So take a good book with you!

On one occasion I had arranged to take some documents from the Portuguese association I worked for, to be signed by the Minister for the Environment, at a set time convenient to him. After waiting over 1 ½ hours I'm afraid I became rather impatient, so I left a curt note saying that I too was a busy person and would he like to contact us when he was free! So even the powers that be are not beyond reproach.

Gifts

Business gifts are acceptable, but keep them discreet, maybe something connected with your own company. Should you be invited for a meal at a Portuguese house, a gift for the hostess is appreciated (chocolates or flowers).

Form of address
When addressing business colleagues remember that anyone with a university degree in Portugal can use the title Doutor ('Doctor') without the same depth of meaning as in the UK. If you are aware of your colleagues' background, then you can address them as Doutor/Doutora, otherwise Senhor/Senhora is acceptable.

WORKING HOURS

Opening hours

Banks:	8.30 am–3 pm (Mon–Fri)
Shops usually:	9 am–1 pm/3 pm–7 pm (Mon–Fri) and 9 am–1 pm (Sat). Large shopping centres usually open from 10am–11pm, even at weekends, as they are often a focus point for socialising.

Public services: 9 am–12.30 pm/ 2 pm–5.30 pm (Mon–Fri). You may find someone available to help you over the lunch hour, but don't expect it.

It is common for factories to begin earlier in the morning, and in all aspects of business, meetings often take place well into the evening. Don't be surprised to find various professions carrying on their work until a late hour. In August most people take their holidays so business slows down considerably.

Meals

Long lunches are common and may be taken as an extension of the business morning. Most people eat out at lunchtime when at work and finding a table can sometimes pose a problem. If you are negotiating a deal of some kind, it is possible for it to be finalised and agreed at a meal so keep a clear head, even though the table is crowded with bottles of wine. Similarly, an evening meal is not uncommon and this can last well into the night. If you are not a wine connoisseur, let your Portuguese colleagues order, rather than choosing a tourist type of drink, and if you are not a smoker be prepared for a nicotine-filled evening, as the Portuguese smoke considerably, especially whilst out eating. Offer to pay the bill, of course, but don't be surprised if your offer is declined. Don't insist on paying it, once your colleague has picked it up.

COMMUNICATING

The ideal situation would be for you to speak Portuguese,

and you should make every effort to learn something, both before you leave the UK and on arrival (see language courses in Chapter 10). Although English is widely spoken, as is French, in business contexts the situation can never be perfect, as misunderstandings through lack of linguistic knowledge could ruin your business chances. Spanish is widely understood, but should be avoided unless you explain first that you do speak Spanish and would they mind you explaining your needs through that language. Be careful though, the misconception that Spanish and Portuguese are almost identical could lead you into disastrous circumstances – the two languages do tend to go off at tangents from time to time.

How to get business done in a foreign environment

◆ learn the language before you go

◆ have a good supply of phrase books and a dictionary

◆ show willing – at least attempt the language, even at an elementary level

◆ apologise for your lack of Portuguese and decide on a common language, be it English, French or Spanish

◆ arrange for interpreters/translators for negotiations and official documents (see list in Useful Contacts).

Communicating in other languages is often great fun but remember if your business or career is at stake, it is vital both parties fully understand each other.

SUCCESS AND FAILURE

Without wanting to put a damper on your hopes and expectations, I think it's only fair to warn you that many people flock to Portugal each year, maybe with the same aspirations as yourself, the attraction of climate and life-style obliterating rational thought and logical reasoning. A great majority of these ex-pats head for the Algarve, knowing that they will be able to get by without any knowledge of the language, and even with few skills should be able to find something to tide them over. Many open bars, seduced by the glamour, the night-life, and the title of landlord. But late hours, the availability of cheap drink and the lack of a disciplined routine has led in recent years to a huge turnover in bar owners. Families break up at an alarming rate, in the Algarve particularly, and very few people have the tenacity to really establish themselves.

But that's not to say the same fate awaits you. The very fact that you are bothering to read this book is a positive factor in your favour. Hopefully you will be more aware of the pitfalls and make provision accordingly. But do consider your family situation as much as any business side to your intended venture. If your partner, for example, has been used to working in the UK and finds his/her position reversed on moving, this can put undue stress upon family relations. But with a bit of foresight and planning, and with enthusiasm and determination, the opportunities do exist.

Good luck!

CHECKLIST

1. Have you done background research into the most suitable area for your business?

2. Have you really thought through what you want to do, and what you could do?

3. Do you have the correct financial and legal advice to guide you in your venture?

4. Have you taken on board the differences in business etiquette and working hours?

5. What efforts have you made to enable you to do business in the right language?

6. Are you being realistic, and have you considered your whole family in this venture?

$$\left(7\right)$$

Dealing with Retirement and Bereavement

If you have decided to retire in Portugal, in order to take advantage of the climate, lifestyle and pace so many of us crave, you need to realise that there are a number of preparatory steps you should take beforehand. Although mobility within the EU is easier now than it ever has been, there is still much careful planning required to ensure your retirement is worry-free. Procedures you need to consider include:

- securing a Residence Permit
- enrolling in the Portuguese social security system
- arranging pension payments
- ensuring adequate health cover
- property purchase, with implications particularly for inheritance after death.

THE PENSION SCHEME IN PORTUGAL
If you are already working in Portugal and paying into the Portuguese social security system, the minimum retirement age is 65 for both men and women. This is when you will become eligible for a state pension to which you have contributed during your working life.

Your national insurance record takes into account periods of absence from work (including sickness, work accidents, maternity leave or unemployment). Pensions are payable only if you can provide evidence that you have paid at least 15 years of contributions (each year requiring at least 120 days of contributions).

State pensions are indexed to take account of rises in the cost of living. In December, pensioners receive a Christmas bonus, and in July, a 14th monthly payment, the amounts of which are equal to those of the pension. The overlapping of an old age pension with occupational earnings is permitted. You need to apply for your pension entitlements about three to four months before the date you plan to retire. For this you will need to complete a pension request form. Contact your regional social security centre (**Centro regional de segurança social, CRSS**) for further details. The regional offices are as follows:

Northern Region: CRSS, Rua Dr.António Patrício 1011, 4151 Porto Codex

Central: CRSS, Rua Padre Estêvão Cabral, 3007 Coimbra Codex

Lisbon area: CRSS, Calç. Engenheiro Miguel Pais, 32, 1294 Lisboa Codex

Alentejo: CRSS, Rua Chafariz d'El Rei 22, 7001 Évora Codex

Algarve: CRSS, Rua Infante D.Henrique, 34, 1-Esq., 8001 Faro Codex.

You may also consult the local offices in your town of residence. For further information you can also contact the

National Pensions Centre: Centro Nacional de Pensões, Campo Grande 6, 1771 Lisboa Codex.

OBTAINING A RESIDENCE PERMIT

As with any EU citizen moving to live in Portugal, you must obtain a **cartão de residência** within three months of your arrival. Details of how to do this are explained in Chapter 4. However, if you are intending to retire to Portugal, you will be asked to produce additional documentation:

◆ Evidence of income – this could be a bank reference which has been translated by an approved translator. You will certainly need proof of all the money at your disposal (including pension entitlements). Enquire at the nearest Portuguese consulate before going to Portugal in order to establish precisely what you will need.

◆ You may also be required to produce a medical certificate. Once again, check this with your local consulate before leaving the UK. Evidence of medical insurance may also be required.

TRANSFERRING HEALTH AND WELFARE RIGHTS

EU citizens are covered by reciprocal arrangements within the EU allowing them to transfer their rights to another member country. Chapter 11 contains information relating to health and disability which may be of interest.

Reaching retirement age

If you have already reached retirement age (60/65), or will have reached retirement age when you move abroad, you need to obtain **Form E121**. To apply for this form in the

UK, write to The Contributions Agency, International Services, Department of Social Security, Longbenton, Newcastle-upon-Tyne, NE98 1YX. The International Services Helpline is (0645) 154811; Fax: (0645) 157800.

You should make arrangements to obtain Form E121 as early as possible before you leave for Portugal. The E121 is valid indefinitely. When you arrive in Portugal, take it to your local or regional Social Security Centre – CRSS. At the same time you must take either your cartão de residência, or the receipt which proves you have applied for it. You will then be enrolled under the Portuguese social security system.

Taking early retirement
If you wish to take early retirement you need to enquire at the Contributions Agency about **Form E106.** This grants healthcare cover for a limited period, after which you will need to make voluntary contributions to the Portuguese system.

Taking out private health insurance
It is a good idea to be a member of a private health insurance scheme even if you have made all the relevant arrangements for transferring your rights under the state systems. If you transfer your rights into the Portuguese system, and subsequently return to the UK and/or fall ill whilst there, no private scheme in the UK will admit or readmit you over the age of 65. You may, then, be left with little cover at just the time of life when you are most likely to need it, or otherwise the prospect of a huge bill for private care.

Remember also that you will not be eligible for any support from the UK government if eventually you are admitted to a private care home or residential home in Portugal.

CLAIMING YOUR PENSION

Claiming a UK retirement pension abroad

If you are entitled to a UK state pension you can ask for a retirement pension forecast from the Contributions Agency. The pension forecast tells you the current level of your pension, and whether or not there are any ways of improving that level. If you are within four months of retirement you will be contacted automatically by the DSS.

You can receive a UK retirement pension, war pension and widows' benefits, in any EU country. The amount you receive will be the same as in the UK, although you should take into account exchange rates. You will also benefit from annual increases in the pension rate if you live within the EU.

You can choose to have the money paid to you:

- directly into your bank account abroad
- into a UK bank or building society
- into the account of a pension of your choice
- sent to your address abroad, either every four or 13 weeks, or annually for small sums.

Claiming pensions from more than one EU country

If you have worked in more than one EU country – for

instance, Portugal and the UK – you will have paid insurance into both systems. Provided you meet the rules of both countries, you will be entitled to a pension from each country's system.

Each country will work out the pension due to you under their own national system. They will also look at the amount of pension due to you from the other country concerned. This can help you to get a pension, or even a higher pension, under their own national system. They do this by working out how much pension you would be entitled to if all your contributions had been paid into one national system.

Until your position is clarified, you receive your pension from each system, according to what you have paid into that system. However, if it is discovered that the total amount of your contributions entitles you to a higher pension, you will eventually receive this without having to ask.

Paying tax on your pension

If you are moving to Portugal from the UK, contact your local tax office in the UK to make arrangements for qualifying as a non-resident, and therefore being exempted from British tax duties. In Portugal you must then contact your local **Finanças Dept.** to register for Portuguese income tax.

BUYING YOUR RETIREMENT HOME

Chapter 3 gives you a basic outline of the process that is involved in purchasing property in Portugal.

Choosing where to buy

When you are trying to decide where to buy your home in Portugal, you should consider a number of issues, especially if you are looking at property in rural areas:

♦ What transport links are there in the vicinity? Do you really want to be in the middle of nowhere? Although isolation from the stresses of our modern world sounds bliss, in reality if something goes wrong you do not want to be that far from the emergency and medical services, as well as being handy for essential shopping. Have you considered what might happen when you are no longer able to get about independently?

♦ Although you may think that 'you want to be alone', you may discover that in fact you want other people nearby. Some parts of Portugal are very sparsely populated indeed, more so in the central and far northern areas, but also parts of the Algarve away from the coast. Whilst this means that you may well be welcomed to an area because you are intending to renovate a derelict property, it could also mean neighbours are very few and far between.

> Portuguese provincial social life is often based on the entertainment of a person's own family. Even if you have a lot of visitors yourself from the UK, this may not really compensate for the lack of social activities to which you are accustomed. Regional ex-patriate associations (see the Regional Directory) may be able to help fill this gap, but not all regions of Portugal offer the same possibilities.

Looking at inheritance issues

It is extremely important that you take good professional advice when buying your property in Portugal, as regards questions of ownership and inheritance. You must do this before you even sign the contracts, afterwards it will be too late. You should also bear in mind that the legal system is excruciatingly slow and can be very expensive in Portugal.

The main thing to watch out for is that the **notário** draws up a contract whereby you buy the property under the married property regime referred to as **separação de bens** (separation of property). The point is important in terms of permission to resell or dispose of the property afterwards. In the event of death an incorrectly stated regime will cause difficulties in winding up the deceased's estate. There may also be issues of Succession Tax. You need to discuss these points with your legal advisers.

DEALING WITH BEREAVEMENT

Although you have all the emotional upheaval to deal with when someone dies, unfortunately there is no escaping the numerous administrative tasks which must also be undertaken. These concern not only winding up a deceased person's estate, but also possibly putting your own affairs in order.

Immediately after the death

1. The death certificate must be signed and certified by a doctor.

2. Within 24 hours of death, the death must be registered at the **Câmara** in the place where the death occurred. For this you need proof of identity, the death

certificate and proof of identity of the deceased (residência, birth or marriage certificate).

3. After registering the death you will be given the official death certificate required by banks and administrative offices etc. Request several copies of the certificate straight away to avoid delays in dealing with the next round of paperwork.

Arranging the funeral

The undertaker can arrange all the certificates as part of the services offered. Before you go ahead with the funeral service you will need a burial permit. Burial is still by far the most common form of funeral in Portugal, and although cremation has now been legalised, so far there is only one crematorium, in Lisbon. Burial usually takes place within 24 hours of the death, so a lot has to be arranged in a very short time.

In addition to the cost of the burial, you will also be faced with a bill for the purchase of a burial plot and tombstone. If you want the burial to take place in the UK make enquiries as to the likely costs involved for transportation. These are likely to be in the region of £2,500, excluding consular fees, flowers and burial notice, depending on the weight of the coffin which will alter the price of the air freight. Although financial assets are officially frozen initially, most banks or financial institutions may release an amount to the immediate family for funeral expenses.

Informing creditors and debtors

The following people must all be notified of a death within a week:

- All banks, savings plans etc, where the deceased had an account. Joint accounts need to be converted into personal accounts.

- Any credit organisations where loans have been taken out.

- All insurance companies, and especially life insurance companies.

- The local health authority, the local pensions unit, and any other welfare units which were issuing benefits to the deceased.

- The landlord if the deceased was renting property. If the deceased was renting his/her property to somebody else, then the tenants must be informed to whom they should now pay their rent.

Wills and inheritance

Normally you will only need to use the services of a **notário** (equivalent to a solicitor) if there is any dispute over the will, or if the deceased was the owner of a property. If the deceased was not a property-owner, and left only furniture, bank accounts etc, then as long as there is no dispute amongst the legatees, there should be no need to involve a notário.

If the deceased owned property you must use a solicitor's services to organise affairs. S/he can undertake various administrative tasks for you which can make life easier at a difficult time. These include dealing with social security offices, the tax offices and tenants. His/her other functions are:

- checking on any unknown claimants on the deceased's estate

- checking the terms of a will

- checking that each legatee has received the correct portion left to him/her under the terms of the will and Portuguese law.

Tax issues

Tax issues are one area where you may well be pleased to benefit from the expertise of a notário, if you are not happy dealing with the tax office yourself. Declaration of inheritance issues are best dealt with the support of legal advice, so that you stay on the right side of the law and the tax office.

One declaration can be made on behalf of all the legatees, and must be made within six months of the death at the tax office of the deceased. Normally any payment due must be made at the same time as the declaration.

Tax declarations have to be made in the name of the deceased (within six months of the death). For the surviving spouse, the tax declaration has to be made at the usual time in the year (March), taking into account revenue acquired between the date of the death and the end of the year. The surviving spouse and any children still benefit from the same number of 'parts' as if the deceased were still alive. For further clarification, speak to your local tax office in Portugal.

COPING ON YOUR OWN

Health and welfare rights for widows and children

If you had Portuguese health and social security rights on account of your late spouse's rights, you and your children will retain these rights, under certain conditions. You should ask for guidance at your local Social Security Centre in order to register for a number of benefits.

Claiming UK widows' benefits

You can continue to receive widows' benefit when you move abroad. Arrangements for transferring this benefit are similar to those for transferring pension payments. Once again, you will receive annual increases to the benefit. To arrange for payment, you must contact The Benefits Agency, Pensions and Overseas Benefits Directorate, Department of Social Security, Tyneview Park, Whitely Road, Benton, Newcastle-upon-Tyne, NE98 1BA. Tel: (0191) 2187777.

You may be entitled to this benefit if your husband dies whilst you were both living abroad if your husband had the necessary National Insurance record in the UK, or if you return to the UK within four weeks of his death.

All the above rules also apply for the payment of widowed mothers' allowance from the UK social security system. However, you cannot claim both benefits – only one or the other.

Claiming Portuguese widows' benefits

If you are widowed in Portugal, and your late spouse was contributing to the Portuguese social security system as an active worker, you will be entitled to a number of financial aids. Information on all the benefits to which you may be entitled can be obtained at your local CRSS or **Centro de Saúde** (Health Centre).

Useful publications available from the Benefits Agency:

+ *A guide to retirement pensions* booklet NP46
+ *Social Security abroad* booklet NI 38
+ *Your social security insurance, benefits and health care rights in the European Community* leaflet SA29.

QUALITY OF LIFE

Despite what appears to be an endless list of concerns, retiring to Portugal is an option many people do successfully take up year after year. Once you have got all your financial/property/health issues in order, you can then expect to enjoy a quality of life that is arguably superior to what you may have experienced previously.

The cost of living is relatively cheaper than in the UK, particularly for food, drink and travel. The pace of life is much more conducive to relaxation. Even if you choose to live in or near the main cities or tourist areas, you can enjoy a slower approach when dealing with the locals, and if you visit some rural locations you might think time has completely stood still.

An important element of society in Portugal is the respect for older people. They are treated with much more deference than in many countries, and if you are following all the earlier advice about integrating into the local community, you will find a particularly warm welcome.

Finally, in general you can enjoy a more clement climate, with a higher rate of average hours of sunshine, but heed the advice in Chapter 11 and be prepared for anything.

CHECKLIST

1. Do you have up-to-date bank statements and other proof of your financial resources ready for your residency application?

2. Have you contacted the appropriate social security agencies to arrange for transfer of pensions and benefits?

3. Have you checked out private healthcare options, and considered which packages offer you the best possibilities?

4. Have you contacted your local tax office to arrange to be declared non-resident?

5. What legal advice do you have in respect of property purchase, wills and tax issues?

6. Are you really clear about where you want to live, and have you weighed up the pros and cons of a particular location first?

⑧

Money Matters

PORTUGUESE BANKS

Most towns have at least a handful of banks, some of the more well-known ones being Banco Totta & Açores, Banco Espírito Santo (one of the wealthiest and most influential families in Portugal), BNU – Banco Nacional Ultramarino, Caixa Geral de Depósitos, as well as Barclays, and until recently, Lloyds (taken over by the Spanish bank Bilbao Vizcaya).

Opening times are generally 8.30 am–3 pm, Monday–Friday, and a full range of services is offered. A table of exchange rates (**câmbio**) is always on display, either in the window or inside, and the clerks can also obtain an up-to-the-minute rate via computer, which they will do anyway should you require money exchange. You will see different rates (**cotação**) displayed for cash (**moeda**) or travellers cheques (**cheques**) and for buying (**compra**) or selling (**venda**).

You will discover that Portuguese banks are very different from those in the UK, in layout and personnel. Usually there is just one long counter, with no security glass panelling, and you will stand at a different section for each type of service you want (typically indicated by a sign on the counter or overhead). One striking feature is that almost exclusively you will be served by a man – it is extremely rare for Portuguese women to work in banks. If your transaction involves receiving money, once the initial paperwork is done, and for câmbio you are required to give your address in Portugal (hotel or otherwise) '**morada em Portugal**' as well as ID, you may then be given a small disc with a number on it. This is your **chapa** and you are required to wait by the **caixa** (till) until your number is called out to indicate your turn. This is quite rare nowadays, as the Portuguese banking system in the main has become so hi-tech, it even has facilities not yet available in the UK.

BANK ACCOUNTS

Once you have decided to stay in Portugal, you will soon need a bank account (**uma conta bancária**). The type you open will depend on your status as a resident, and whether you want a personal or company account.

Residents

If you have been an official resident for a year, having been granted residency by the **Serviço de Estrangeiros**, you may apply for an account, current or deposit (**corrente/depósito a prazo**). Both of these pay interest, and charge tax at source, as you will be used to in the UK. A cheque book will be issued on request and your account will function as in the UK, with automatic machine cards, statements and other usual facilities. You will have to pay a minimum initial amount to start the account.

Non-residents

As a non-resident, you can open a current foreign account with a cheque book, but unless you have the prior consent of the Bank of Portugal, you will not be entitled to interest. To qualify for this type of account, you must have:

◆ Residence Visa or passport
◆ work permit and employer's letter
◆ fiscal number
◆ minimum deposit.

You are considered a foreign resident until you have completed one year of residence.

Foreign currency accounts

Both residents and non-residents may also open an account in a foreign currency. Usually there is a minimum initial deposit (approximately US$1000 or equivalent), and there are restrictions on length of duration. Interest will be paid, but no cheque book is available.

Company accounts

If you/your company are resident you will open a company account as any Portuguese business would, but a non-resident company may also open an account. For both situations a lot of paperwork is necessary, as the bank will require copies of minutes from your company meeting when it was decided to open an account/who can cash cheques/signatures/amounts/memorandum and Articles of Association.

For detailed information on all kinds of bank accounts you can contact any of the banks listed at the end of the book, before leaving the UK.

Electronic Banking

Multibanco is the recent, generic expression used throughout Portugal for the automatic cash machines (known as ATMs in the UK). You can use the machines to undertake banking transactions – order new cheques, request a balance or make deposits, as well as withdraw cash. But you can also pay utilities and Internet bills through them and even buy train tickets. The cards can also be used at most retail outlets to pay for goods and services. The card is swiped through a machine and you confirm the amount and key your pin number into a small device. Some of the cards serve a dual purpose as credit/debit cards and you must make clear when you purchase anything this way that you state whether the transaction is via credit card or bank account.

To obtain a Multibanco card, you simply apply at your bank for the relevant forms. It may take about three weeks to process. The cards have a shelf-life of 12 months, after which they are renewed automatically. This is something to remember, especially if you only spend part of the year in Portugal. Recent visitors forgot their card had expired and tried to use it in a Multibanco, only to have it swallowed before their eyes. Should this happen to you, you need to contact your branch immediately, informing them of the machine that ate your card. You ought to be able to have your card back the same day, however if you do not report it swiftly you may have a wait of around a month to get it back. You can use the cards in any Multibanco machine, regardless of which bank you have your account with. If your card has an Electron symbol on it, it can only be used electronically, and not as a debit card in shops.

USING YOUR NEW ACCOUNT

Cheques

Cheque books (**um livro de cheques**) are usually not books at all, but plastic wallets full of individual cheques, all numbered in order. Accompanying them is a sheet of paper to record your transactions, which acts as your stub, or **talão**. It is essential, then, that you keep your cheques in order and that you don't lose the paper. Keeping an extra copy in another place is always prudent. (See Fig. 14, p. 135.)

How to fill in a blank cheque:

Banco ABC	cheque No
	Pague por este cheque, EUROS
	€100
	The amount in numbers
Assinaturas	Local de emissão
	Oporto
Paulo da Costa	Your branch
Your signature	data
	02/06/23
	N.B. Year/month/day
à ordem de *ESCOLA DE CONDUÇÃO CONFAC*	
payee	
a quantia de *Cem euros*	
Amount in words	

Fig. 13. Filling in a cheque.

Legally you can write your cheque in any language – it will still be presented for payment even if it is not in Portuguese. If you should write a cheque which 'bounces' be careful: three bounces and your bank may ban you from writing cheques at any bank in Portugal for a period of two years. Some banks may phone you to warn you your balance is a bit low, but they are not obliged to do so.

CRÉDITO PREDIAL PORTUGUÊS, S.A.

Sede Social: Rua Augusta, 237   1100 LISBOA
Matriculada na C.R.C. de Lisboa sob o n.º 1587   Contribuinte n.º 500 844 321
Capital Social 30.000.000.000$00   Internet: WWW.CPP.PT

CURRENT ACCOUNT
CONTA CORRENTE

data / DATE	n.º de cheque / CHEQUE Nº	descrição / TRANSACTION	saídas / PAYMENTS	entradas / DEPOSITS	saldo / BALANCE
20/06/08	113	Mr. Silva – car	3,560 00		10,420 00

Fig. 14. Bank account transactions sheet.

Deposits

To make a deposit **(depósito)** you will have to fill in a form **(talão)** such as the example in Figure 15.

Balance

If you want to know your balance **(o saldo)** then simply enter your bank and ask to do so. 'Queria saber o saldo da conta

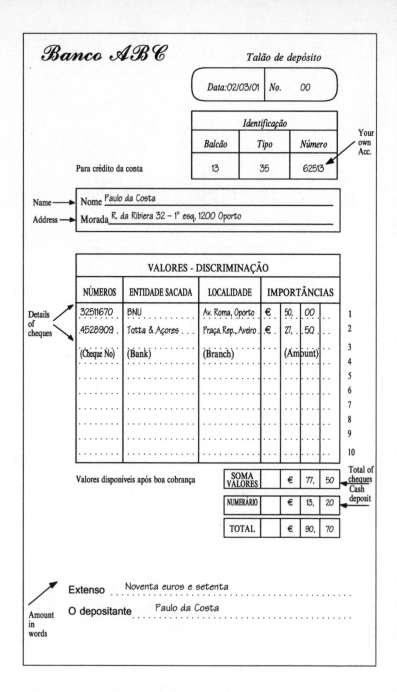

Fig. 15. Filling in a deposit slip.

número..., se faz favor'. You may need proof of ID so always have something with you.

Other transactions

◆ You may need to cash a cheque that has been made out to you. You can only do this by taking it to the drawer's bank, the branch address on the cheque, and you must have ID. You need to ask 'Queria levantar este cheque, se faz favor'. Of course you can also use this expression when drawing cash from your own account.

◆ To order a new book of cheques: 'Queria requisitar um livro de cheques'. Requisitar is the verb to use when you need to order/demand something.

PAYING BILLS

If you choose to pay your bills via your bank account, you can set up a standing order in the same way as in the UK. The company will give you a form (**ficha**) to fill in with your bank details, which will be sent to your branch as a request for **transferência bancária**. When you receive your **factura/recibo** (invoice/receipt) a note will remind you of the debit and will inform you of when this will take place. For example:

vai ser debitada a partir de 02-02-06, através da sua conta bancária No... do banco ABC + branch code...

means

It will be debited after 6th Feb, 2002, through your account number ... at ABC bank.

Should you wish to cancel a debit mandate, you must inform your own bank that you no longer require the payments to be made. Remember you can also pay your bills via the Multibanco.

INTERPRETING BANK STATEMENTS

A monthly statement of your account (**extracto de conta**) will normally be sent to your home.

Another way of checking your transactions is to use the Multibanco machines.

If you think there has been an error on your account, or if there is a transaction/charge you don't understand, then take all the necessary documentation into your bank and (politely) explain the situation to them. There will always be somebody available who speaks English, so if you feel out of your depth trying to establish what has gone wrong in Portuguese, then ask for help in English. They are usually very obliging, but be prepared to wait.

IMPORTING FUNDS

Personal funds

Importation of funds can be undertaken on a personal or a business level. On a personal level, if you find yourself short of money, funds can be transferred either from an existing account in the UK, direct to your Portuguese account, or an individual can arrange for money to be sent out to you, if the quantity is not excessive. You will have to arrange via your bank in Portugal for the funds to be received and deposited into your account. There will be a fee for the service, and the funds will be converted at the rate existing at the time of the transfer. Do check what the fees are going to be, and remember you will also probably be charged by your own UK bank.

If you only need a small amount of money to tide you over, it will probably work out cheaper to have it sent out as an **International Money Order**, which you can cash at a post office. Ask at your local post office about these and the Girobank facilities for sending money abroad. I wouldn't recommend cash being sent out to you, although I did successfully both send and receive cash by disguising it within some sheets of paper before putting it in a strong envelope and sending it by registered post. It is a risk though, so do be careful.

Company funds

When setting up your business you will no doubt need to transfer funds from an existing UK bank account as initial capital investment. This is all part and parcel of the procedure for establishing a business, already mentioned in the previous chapter. The Bank of Portugal has established a total liberalisation of movements of capital, in line with the latest EU legislation. Now, more than at any other previous time, transfer of funds has been facilitated, and a business may apply to import funding with confidence. However, the procedure still remains a rigorous pile of paperwork, and the Bank of Portugal continues to reserve the right to deny a transaction, on each case's merits. Always check with financial consultants before you enter into any procedure.

INVESTING OFFSHORE

Most people will, at some time or other, have heard of the idea of investing funds in an offshore tax haven; the usual places being Jersey, Gibraltar or the Isle of Man. But how does it work and why do it? If you are buying property in Portugal (or any country), the possibility of doing so through an offshore company means that a variety of financial benefits may be enjoyed. What happens is that an offshore company is created, through financial arrangers, shares for which are registered in the names of nominees holding those shares in trust for the owner. Although it sounds rather complicated, it is relatively easy to set up, so long as you check out the credentials of any potential adviser. In the wake of recent financial scandals which left hundreds of investors without money, confidence in financial investments has dipped slightly; however, many people do buy their property this way, enjoying the following benefits:

◆ loan facility with a longer duration
◆ avoidance of capital gains tax, on resale of property
◆ avoidance of inheritance taxes
◆ ease of transfer of property to heirs
◆ limited liability.

Offshore company services generally offer a full range of financial investment suggestions, but you should shop around before accepting any. Some companies have representatives in the UK, who can guide you in the right direction.

See list in Useful Contacts section.

NB. Consider this option very carefully, and with expert advice, as changes imposed by a new Portuguese law are making this a less attractive option.

PREPARING BUSINESS ACCOUNTS

If you are self-employed or intend to open a business in Portugal, you will require the services of a creditable firm of accountants in order to prepare your books at the end of the financial year. The books pertaining to your business must be kept for a minimum of 10 years. Companies must submit the following documents:

- ◆ balance sheet
- ◆ profit and loss account
- ◆ notes to the financial statements
- ◆ statement of source and application of funds.

Small businesses are only required to prepare a balance sheet and profit and loss account. The National Committee of Accounting Standards (**Comissão de normalização contabilista**) has set accounting norms in a range of areas, including timeshare activities, and accounts for individual income taxes. The introduction of an official chart of accounts (**plano oficial de contas**) setting out accounting principles, means that the accounting system is rigorously adhered to. It is vital that you keep your books and all documents (invoices, receipts...) in order yourself throughout the year, to avoid handing over a headache for your accountants to sort out.

Find yourself a reputable accountancy firm (**contabilistas**) by asking around, or choose from the list at the end of this book. Large firms such as Arthur Andersen, Coopers & Lybrand, Touche Ross, Price Waterhouse, and Ernst & Young will all issue advice in the form of booklets, or will arrange an interview with you in the UK. You may find that a smaller local firm will offer the service you require and probably at a fraction of the price. For additional information on Portuguese banking and finance, check out the website of the *Financial Times*: http/surveys.ft.com/2002

THE DESPACHANTE

The **despachante** is almost a mythical figure in the Portuguese-speaking world. He is the man who gets things done, the waver of the magic wand, who miraculously weaves his way through mounds of paperwork. This worker of wonders will all but pay your car fine and get your house built – for a small fee of course!

The despachante works as intermediary in all official negotiations and transactions. If you haven't the time, or patience/tolerance, to go dashing about from one department to another, looking for people to translate, validate and stamp your documents, then by depositing all your papers with a despachante you will have the perspiration taken out of the procedure. Even so you will no doubt have to be called in at various times to sign papers or bring further evidence/documentation, which somebody omitted to tell you about initially. But eventually things do get done. The despachante is well worth knowing. Not always easy to locate, there is rarely an obvious office. You will have to ask around to find one, and try and chat to people who may have used his services, so you get an idea of quality, efficiency and price.

CHECKLIST

1. Do you have the necessary documents and deposit to open the relevant bank account?

2. Have you applied for your Multibanco card?

3. Do you know how to fill in cheques, stubs and deposit slips?

4. Have you investigated the pros and cons of offshore investment?

5. Are you meticulously keeping accounts up to date?

6. Do you know where to find the despachante?

9

Driving in Portugal

DOCUMENTS

If you are visiting Portugal as a temporary visitor (up to six months) you may drive using your current UK licence, international licence or the new pink EU licence which some people have been issued with. Once you have become a resident in Portugal if you have an EU licence this is valid, otherwise once your UK licence expires you must obtain a Portuguese licence. You do this by applying at the local traffic department, **Direcção de Viação** (your town hall will be able to direct you to the relevant place), and producing all relevant documentation (personal and vehicular, and don't forget to take photocopies as well).

Some organisations are recommending that people photocopy the following extract and keep it with their driving documents, as recent confusion surrounding driving licences has lead to this clarification:

Extrato do Guia emitido pelo Ministério da Administração Interna, Direcção Geral de Viação, datado 5 de Agosto 1996.
'A partir do dia 1 de Julho de 1996, será adoptado um 'modelo normalizado' de carta de condução com vista a facilitar a sua compreensão e reconhecimento mútuo.

Qualquer carta de condução emitada por um Estado-Membro é reconhecida pelos outros Estados-membros, independentemente de se tratar de uma carta recente... ou de uma carta antiga, desde que se encontre dentro do seu prazo de validade. Por conseguinte, deixa de ser obrigado a trocar a sua carta de condução original por uma carta do Estado-Membro de acolhimento quando se instalar nesse outro Estado-Membro.'

Translated, this means: Extract of the Directive issued by the Internal Administration Ministry, Driving Licence Centre, dated 5 August 1996. 'As of 1 July 1996, a 'standard model' for driving licences will be adopted so as to facilitate understanding and mutual recognition. Any driving licence issued by a Member State is to be recognised by other Member States, regardless of the age of the licence as long as it is valid. Consequently, it is now no longer compulsory to exchange an original driving licence for a licence issued by the new Member State when one chooses to reside in that new Member State.' Different regulations apply to non-EU citizens.

Insurance

You can obtain the international insurance certificate (green card) from any insurers before you leave the UK which will cover you whilst in Portugal. Ordinary car insurance is also easily obtainable once within the country, from any insurance company (**companhia de seguros**). The best thing would be to enquire where other ex-pats have obtained theirs. For shorter-term cover, check with your own insurers for extended warranty for Europe, especially for roadside recovery, which can add hundreds of pounds to the cost of breakdown problems. The AA reckons that one in 26 motorists need breakdown assistance whilst abroad.

Tax

If you are bringing in your own car, then it must display a current tax disc. In Portugal car tax is only applicable to new vehicles or those recently imported and depends on engine size. The car tax year runs from January to December. The media usually announce when car tax stamps are available; they can be bought from certain shops for a short time, then from the Finanças offices.

MOT

Inspections are needed for cars over 4 years old, according to when they were first registered. Inspections should then be every other year, then annually when the car is over 8 years old.

Registration documents

Again, if you are bringing in your own car, you must have the relevant, valid registration (ownership) papers. If you are borrowing a friend's car you should have a letter of authorisation to drive it, and ideally it should have been officially recognised by the Portuguese Consulate General.

Always check with the Consulate General if in any doubt as to your position.

IMPORTING A VEHICLE

If you take a foreign registered car into Portugal, and intend to stay only as a temporary resident/visitor, you may keep the car there for up to six months. There is a possibility of an extension on this period, but you would have to have a good reason for being in the country for so long. Once you become a resident, then your car should be taken out of the country after six months or you must go through the lengthy and expensive process of importing it. Before you leave the UK with your vehicle, you should contact the Vehicle Licensing Office with details of your intended departure, and they will issue you with a certificate of export. You must display GB stickers on your vehicle.

Import

If you want to import your car permanently, either initially or once you are established, there are certain points you should bear in mind:

♦ As the Portuguese drive on the right, your own car will not be geared up for efficient driving, leaving you at a disadvantage, especially for overtaking.

♦ If the car is to be used only for personal use and not for business purposes then the usual import tax may not be applicable, but as there are certain conditions which determine this, you need to have this verified by the Portuguese Consulate in the UK.

♦ The process is long and complex, so this should be kept in mind, depending on your need for the car. The Portuguese authorities have, however, now agreed that if a vehicle owner wants to drive their vehicle in another EU Member State during the registration procedure s/he can ask for the 'temporary restitution of the original registration document'. This was in response to pressure from the European Commission, following many complaints about the tardy registration process.

Buying

Cars are generally more expensive in Portugal, although there are plenty of second-hand vehicles around. Buying a diesel-engined car is a good bet, as diesel is significantly cheaper than petrol. Check all ownership documents very carefully before you take over a vehicle.

CAR RENTAL

To rent a car in Portugal you must be over 23 and have held a full licence for over 12 months. Rental can be arranged via a holiday/rental firm before you leave the UK, should you require a reserved car on arrival, or at any time whilst in the country from one of the company branches situated around the country. Avis, Budget, Europcar and Hertz all have main branches in the airports and main cities, with agents operating in other areas. Their distinctive signs are easy to find. In the *Yellow Pages* look under Automóveis/carros...aluguel = hire/rental.

The price of rental will depend on:

- type/size of car
- length of rental period – usually better discounts for longer period
- supply of petrol in tank – if the tank is full when you collect, you may be expected to return it as such
- collect/deposit location – some companies allow you to collect the car at one place, and leave it at another of

their offices, for which there is a fee levied

♦ season – some discounts are offered in low season.

Any travel operator will inform you of relevant details. Alternatively you may have a local car rental firm to check information with.

DRIVING IN GENERAL

You have heard people complain that the Italians/Belgians/Greeks are mad drivers, but what of the Portuguese? Those of us who have lived to tell the tale can also add these usually unassuming people to the list of potential rally drivers, once behind the wheel. They just seem so unaware of danger, and often travel at high speeds, overtaking round corners, so you really have to keep your wits about you if you are driving. I was once sitting in the back of a car driven by a Portuguese teacher who constantly turned round to talk to me, completely taking his eyes off the road. In the end I pretended not to listen so he would give up and concentrate on the road ahead!

Whilst driving in Portugal it is obligatory to carry with you at all times:

♦ a valid driving licence
♦ ID (passport or Residência)
♦ log book (**livrete**) or rental contract
♦ valid vehicle insurance.

If you are stopped by police you must be able to produce all of these.

Roads

The quality of roads varies enormously. The smaller country roads, like our B roads and some A roads, can be impossible – full of pot holes, inadequately signposted and poorly surfaced. Main roads through towns and joining cities are better, especially the larger **estradas** and **estrada nacional**. The upgraded EN roads are now known as IPs (**itinerário principal**). These are more like our dual carriageways and form the major link between North, South, East and West. They are designated by numbers, for example, the EN125 which crosses the Algarve, and the EN264 which goes up to Lisbon from the South. There are a few real motorways (**auto-estradas**), the main ones being around Lisbon, Oporto and Braga; they function as toll roads. Probably the most used stretch so far is from the South over the April 25th bridge into Lisbon, where traffic congestion in the summer, at weekends and rush hour is horrendous. It can sometimes take up to 2 hours to cross the bridge. A new bridge, the Vasco da Gama, has been built slightly upstream from the original. The new A2 motorway from Lisbon to the Algarve became fully operational in July 2002, despite a number of protests from environmental groups over the negative impact on the surrounding countryside.

Remember
Driving is on the right, overtaking therefore is on the left and priority is given to the right. This is particularly important on roundabouts, unless indicated otherwise.

For road signs and commands see further on.

DRIVING LESSONS/TEST

You may take lessons in Portugal, and the test involves both practical driving, and a written test (similar to our road sign/highway code test). You do have to have a thorough medical before the licence is issued. You must see a doctor, who will test vision, heart, general body ability, nervous system, and check your 'estado mental' – mental state!

If you have passed without any major problem, the doctor will fill in a certificate, which you will take back to the Driving Centre to be assessed, along with your actual test.

Once you have passed the whole ordeal, you will be issued with a Portuguese licence, like the EU licence available now.

LAWS OF THE ROAD

One of the worst aspects of driving in Portugal is that the laws relating to vehicles are constantly changing, therefore almost everyone, at some point or other, finds themselves on the wrong side of the law, and usually for a very petty reason. For example, one clamp down was on the height of vehicle mudflaps from the road. People were fined for not having the flap at a certain height, whilst other much more serious transgressions were ignored. Completely illogical, and very frustrating.

General rules

◆ Seat belts are obligatory at all times, and children under 12 are supposed to travel in the back.

◆ The legal alcohol limit is 0.4g per litre. A big campaign

was launched against drinking and driving (Bebeu? Não conduza! Have you had a drink? Don't drive!), yet, despite this, and steep penalties for contravention it is surprising just how many people (both foreigners and nationals) continue to drive home after an evening meal where large amounts of alcohol have been consumed.

♦ All vehicles should carry a first-aid box and a red warning triangle – to be erected on the road in the event of breakdown.

♦ Speed limits – 50 kph (30mph) in built-up areas/90kph (56mph) on open roads/120kph (74mph) on motorways. For bigger vehicles such as lorries and coaches, the limits are approximately 20% lower.

♦ If you have been driving for less than a year, you must observe a 90kph limit, and must also display a sticker at the back of the vehicle (available from the Portuguese Automobile Club).

Motorcycle riders are obliged to wear a helmet although, looking at some of the old-fashioned styles around which are not even strapped on, this rule seems irrelevant in terms of safety.

Bicycles – you should have a licence, either from home or from the local council (**câmara**). You will notice bicycles have a small matriculation plate.

If you are a member of AFPOP, the foreign property-owners association (address in Useful Contacts), their newsletters tend to inform of latest legislative changes relating to vehicles, as do the English language newspapers.

THE POLICE

There are four police forces functioning, all of which can deal with traffic problems and offences. The ones you will most often see all over the country are the austere-looking, armed GNR **(Guarda Nacional Republicana)**, dressed in grey uniforms and often patrolling the streets in pairs. They often go out on country roads as routine practice, stopping vehicles at whim and demanding to see documents. Often very awkward to deal with, they can be unrelenting if there is just one slight detail out of order with your papers. The GNR have their own station in towns, usually with the Portuguese flag outside, and are very military.

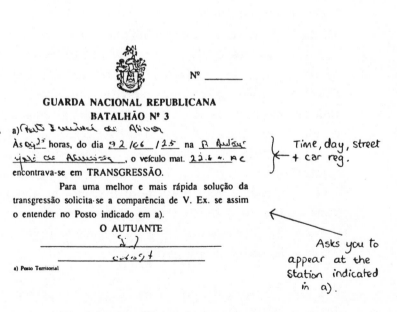

Fig. 16. Ticket issued by police.

Another police headquarters will be that of the more common **Polícia (de Segurança Pública) PSP** – the public safety police, who deal with a range of more administrative services, as well as controlling traffic. They have a dark blue uniform, again armed, and seem to have a bit more spark about them than the GNR.

Finally there is the Traffic Brigade, **Brigâda de Tránsito**, who deal specifically with motoring problems such as speeding, disputes, delays.

To complete the picture, there are also the **Guarda Fiscal**, who are a customs and excise patrol, controlling borders and coastal areas.

Make sure when driving that you have all relevant documents, that the car is in order (although if police in any country want to be difficult, they'll find something wrong), and that you are polite. Don't try and offer bribes to get out of a situation; invariably the police will take your money and book you anyway. If you are given a fine, usually to be taken and paid at the nearest police HQ, which you believe is unwarranted, find somebody who speaks Portuguese to go with you and explain the situation. If all else fails a Consulate official may be able to show you how to appeal, but the legal system takes so long to proceed (some cases wait 3–5 years to come to court), you may be better off just paying up.

You may find a ticket, see Figure 16, on your car which does not tell you what you have done wrong, but asks you to appear at the station indicated to solve the problem. It is highly likely to be a parking offence.

CAMPING AND CARAVANNING

There is an extensive network of camping and caravanning parks across the country, all well serviced and mostly in beautiful wooded areas or within easy access of beaches. Casual overnight stops on roadsides or in the country are prohibited. However, you may stop for a reasonable amount of time on a motorway service station to cook a meal.

Camp sites

Camp sites are very cheap, some working out at little more than a pound or two per night, although parking and caravans have an extra charge, still very low. There are four classes of site, almost as a star category in a hotel, but in addition there are private P parks where only members of that particular association may stay. There are also two types of general parks: those which belong to certain clubs or to the Portuguese Camping and Caravanning Federation – only foreign visitors holding an International FICC card may use them – and free sites, where usually a passport will suffice for entry.

Most sites have excellent facilities, but remember, if you are camping in the summer months, the wooded, sandy locations are also the resting place of irksome insects, so be well protected. A useful publication giving information on all the camp sites is the **Roteiro campista** (camping guide) available from most bookshops/kiosks in Portugal.

Further information is available from the Portuguese

Trade and Tourism Office in London, or the Camping Club of Great Britain. Tel: (01203) 694995. Also on: http://www.roteiro-campista.pt or info@roteiro-campista.pt

ROAD SIGNS

Many of the road signs are similar to, if not the same as, those you may be accustomed to in the UK. Obviously a working knowledge of the language is essential for you to understand all signs you may be confronted with, but the list below contains some of the most common.

Curva perigosa	Dangerous bend
Acenda as luzes	Switch on headlights
Conduza com cautela	Drive carefully
Dê prioridade	Give way
Sentido único	One way
Cruzamento	Crossroad
Devagar	Slow
Desvio	Diversion
Pare	Stop
Olhe	Look
Estacionamento proibido	No parking
Passagem de nível	Level crossing
Parque de estacionamento	Car park
Proibida a ultrapassagem	No overtaking
Prioridade à direita	Give way to the right

BREAKDOWN SERVICES

If you break down on the motorway, you will find emergency phones on the hard shoulder, as in the UK. However, as the motorway system is still very small, you are more likely to need to use an ordinary phone to get assistance. If you are a member of a motoring organisation such as AA or RAC, you may seek help from the **Portuguese Automobile Club (ACP)**. Its breakdown service in Lisbon can be contacted at R. General Humberto Delgado No. 3, 2685-340 Prior Velho, Lisboa. Tel: 21 942 91 03.

If you are further north, contact Travessa da Prelada 453/463, 4250-380 Oporto. Tel: 22 834 00 01. They have branches throughout the country and include the following additional breakdown services.

Braga Tel: 253 217051	Aveiro Tel: 234 422571
Coimbra Tel: 239 852020	Faro Tel: 289 898950
Évora Tel: 266 707533	Guarda Tel: 271 213467

If you are not a member of any automobile association, you will have to resign yourself to the relentless search for a repair garage (**oficina de reparação**), but remember, very few open at the weekend. (See Glossary for a list of vehicle terms.) Some service stations (**estação de serviço**) may help out, but the service will be limited and again, they are rarely open at weekends.

FUEL
Filling stations (**posto de gasolina**) are very well represented throughout the country, either the large companies such as GALP (Portuguese) and BP which in larger cities and motorways usually open all night, or the smaller businesses, some with just one or two pumps (**bombas**), whose service hours do not extend past the late evening. Be careful defining what type of fuel you require, as hundreds of

tourists each year get it wrong and swamp their engines with diesel.

gasolina = petrol ⎱ normal = 2 star
                        ⎰ super = 4 star
                            sem chumbo = unleaded

Gasóleo = diesel
Óleo = oil

Petrol is served in litres.

USEFUL INFORMATION

Via Verde

There are now a number of toll roads in Portugal, and in order to avoid delays in queues waiting to pay the toll, you can apply at the tollbooths for a special device called a **Via Verde** which speeds up your passage. It is, in fact, a box with a magnetic strip which you fix to the windscreen of your car. When you approach the toll booths you can go through the **Linha Verde** fast lanes without stopping by swiping your Multibanco card through the device. The tolls are then automatically deducted from your bank account and you will receive a monthly statement. Obviously, then, you need both a bank account and a card in order to take advantage of the scheme.

Speed reduction traffic lights

Portugal's reputation as one of the most dangerous countries to drive in has jolted it into an initiative on some of the danger-hot spots, such as the 'Marginal' (between Lisbon and Cascais), considered the worst road stretch in Europe for accidents. Special traffic lights have been installed which can pick up, through sensors, if a car is exceeding the speed limit. This will turn the lights to red, and if you fail to stop you may be banned for between a month and a year, and also receive a fine. It remains to be seen whether this will lower the number of horrendous incidents on these roads, but the scheme is to be welcomed.

Car insurance
Third party insurance is compulsory in Portugal (and no wonder!). Contact any local insurance broker for details. See Useful Contacts section.

The Portuguese AA – Automóvel Club de Portugal (ACP)
The Club issues a range of advice and maps, and is very friendly and helpful. They can guide you on the tricky business of importing your car, plus services such as:

* breakdown and recovery
* driving lessons
* discounts on travel-related goods and holidays
* insurance
* camping and caravanning
* driving licences
* monthly magazine
* car hire
* legal services.

ACCIDENTS
If you have a minor car accident, and both parties agree on where the blame lies, you do not have to call the police and you are allowed to move your vehicles out of danger to other road users. Both parties need to complete a European Accident Statement – **Declaração Amigável de Acidente Automóvel** – (issued by your insurance company,

and best left in the car). Both parties must sign the form together, then you send the copy to your insurance company to sort out.

However, if you are involved in a more serious accident, or if there is a dispute over the blame, then you should call the police. Do not attempt to move the car until they arrive, as you may be removing evidence. Remember to put your red triangle on the road as a warning of hazard to other road users. The police will take statements from witnesses and these, together with any police reports, will be sent to the respective insurance companies to sort out. There is a Compensation Board for claims against uninsured drivers, but your insurance company or the police will advise you.

Always remember, when out in your car, to check you have with you all the relevant documents relating to the vehicle (driving licence, insurance certificate, ownership documents, the green log book, plus the blue registration papers).

CHECKLIST

1. Do you have all the relevant documents which will allow you to drive in Portugal?

2. Have you properly considered either importing your vehicle, or buying one in Portugal?

3. Are you fully insured for driving?

4. Are you familiar with Portuguese driving laws?

5. Do you have a list of emergency contact numbers?

6. Are you clear about accident procedures?

(10)

Education

PORTUGUESE SYSTEM

Read any Portuguese publication about its own education system and it will probably talk of 'education reform'; a step in the right direction after many years of unrest, disruptions and stilted progress. Despite the positive outlook, progress, as always, is taking its time, although EU funding is now providing many more opportunities for vocational training schemes in particular.

The problems

These recently have included high rates of student absenteeism, coupled with equally high numbers of teachers failing to turn up at lessons. In rural areas, particularly, young people prefer and are expected to help at home on the land, and education is still not seen as a priority by many families. Working conditions, long hours and low pay have resulted in dissatisfaction amongst teachers. Some schools are overcrowded for their size, and here a dual system occurs, with some pupils having only morning lessons, and some only in the afternoon. There is a significant lack of materials, including books, and many schools appear to be much more basic in their design and structure than in the UK. The school-leaving age is 15.

PORTUGAL

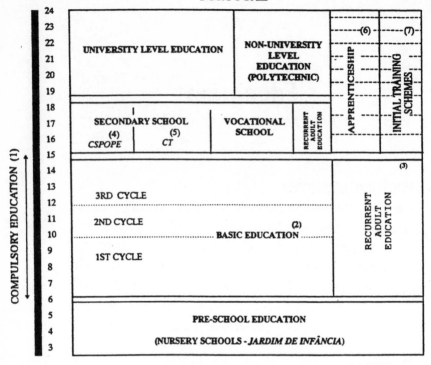

1. Until 1987, compulsory education in Portugal lasted 6 years, whilst compulsory attendance lasted until 14 years of age (i.e. 8 years). The Comprehensive Law on the Education System of October 1986 extended compulsory education to 9 years - applicable to pupils enrolled in the first year of basic education for the 1987/88 school year and for subsequent school years.

2. Basic Education comprises compulsory education of 9 years, consisting of three consecutive cycles of 4, 2 and 3 years respectively, and is roughly equivalent to primary and lower secondary level.

3. 3-year evening courses of general or technical education for early school leavers and adults.

4. Secondary courses predominantly leading to further studies (*Cursos Secundários Predominantemente Orientados para o Prosseguimento de Estudos - CSPOPE,*) or general courses;

5. Secondary courses predominantly oriented towards working life, or technological courses (*Cursos Tecnológicos - CT*).

6. Apprenticeship is accessible to young people aged 14 to 24. It lasts 1 to 4 years.

7. Initial training schemes in various employment sectors, of various lengths.

⋯⋯⋯⋯⋯⋯ = division in the level/type of education

– – – – – – – – = alternative beginning or end of level/type of education

Fig. 17. The Portuguese Education System;
from European Commission DG XXII: Education, Training and Youth.

Advantages

Putting your child into the Portuguese system can have its advantages, and none more so than the language factor. Although bewildering at first, you'll be surprised how quickly your child picks up the language, which will enable a faster integration into the society. The Portuguese curriculum includes a study of philosophy, confined in the UK to older students, and most Portuguese students have claimed how interesting and valuable a subject it is. State schools are free, but places in many are limited. Aim to visit prospective local Portuguese schools.

Higher education is not as organised or on anything like the same scale as in the UK.

BRITISH SCHOOLS

British (or American) schools exist in the larger towns where ex-pats live. They are mostly centred around the Algarve, Lisbon and Oporto and are usually known as International schools because of the pupil mix of nationalities (UK, German, Danish, Chinese...). Apart from the American school in Lisbon, which follows the US high school system, the British-run schools follow the British curriculum, offering the same GCSEs and a very limited number of A levels. All are fee-paying, a factor which should be taken into consideration, although some may offer bursaries and scholarships.

Great care should be exercised when choosing an International school, as some are notoriously badly run, inefficient, and have an abysmal attitude to children's education. The example at the end of this chapter illustrates how insufficient experience of running an educational establishment, lack of communication amongst staff/parents/owners can lead to a complete disaster, and could ruin your child's important years of education.

Spotting the pitfalls
But how do you know how to spot the pitfalls?

♦ The best first step is to visit as many as you can, asking for details of the school's history, and that of its staff. Study any literature the school gives you, but read between the lines – school prospectuses often boost the image of what could be a shoddy establishment working from apartments.

♦ Try to speak to present and past pupils and parents.

♦ Look out for recommended schools listed in publications such as that of the European Council of International Schools, ECIS.

♦ Gather as much information as you can before taking a decision which could affect your child for the rest of his or her life.

UK BOARDING
One of the considerations to weigh up if you are planning an upheaval abroad is how that uprooting will interrupt and affect your child's education, particularly if they are in the middle of important school years. How quickly could they readjust to a new environment/language/lifestyle/school; can they wrench themselves from friends and start again? Many parents make the decision of going because they fancy it, or have to (company move, or for less noble

reasons!), without considering that their child's potential can be ruined if they don't adapt quickly. Remember that not all International schools have your child's best interests at heart.

One option many families are faced with is that of leaving the child in the UK to carry on their studies until a convenient change can be made. Whatever your preconceived ideas on boarding schools they do offer a solution to a major problem. If fees are a stumbling block, remember that all International schools in Portugal are also fee-paying, so it's worth comparing prices and relative values for education.

If you, or your child, is worried about life on their own, why not pursue the possibility of their staying with relatives or friends until their schooling is over – that way they can continue in familiar surroundings without interruption to studies and they will have the security of familiar faces at home. There are always the school holidays for them to visit you. And don't forget if you and Portugal don't hit it off, what a blow that would be if you have taken your child out of their UK school, only to return in one or two years.

Each child is different of course, and only you, and they, will really know what will be suitable; just be aware of the pitfalls in each option.

PRIMARY SCHOOLING
If you have young children, the choice again is yours, as to whether a Portuguese or an International school is most

appropriate. Pre-primary schooling in the state system is fairly scant, but there is a growing number of private kindergartens around. Primary education itself starts at age six, and lasts four years. Many of the International primary schools base their teaching around the Montessori style environment (a child-centred basis for sense stimulation through play without real rigid discipline), so you must also consider what kind of schooling you wish for your child, and what he or she requires.

Some of the larger International secondary schools also have a primary section, which can be useful if you have children of varying ages. However, students I have spoken to who have been at International schools have commented that by the time they have passed from primary to 5th form in the same school establishment, they felt ready for a change. This then could lead to disruption at 16 + if your child did not want to stay on at the same school. On the other hand, many children just get on with their schooling without really noticing. A typical private primary school may cost in the region of £300 + per term.

International primary schools worth contacting are:

Montessori International School, 'Miraventos' Estrada de Oeiras 22, Porto Salvo 2780 Oeiras (nr Lisbon). Tel: 21 421 2848.

St Laurence International school (see next section).

Colégio de Vilamoura (see next section).

Boa Ventura Montessori School, Rua Nunes dos Santos, 5, 2765 São Pedro do Estoril. Tel: 21 468 8023.

The International Prep. School, Rua do Boror 12, Carcavelos, 2775 Parede (nr Lisbon). Tel: 21 457 0149 (member of ECIS).

St Georges School, Av. do Lidador, 32, São João do Estoril, 2765 Estoril. Tel: 21 466 1774.

The Cascais International school, Rua das Faias, Lt. 7
Torre, 2750 Cascais. Tel: 21 484 6260 (Montessori
based).

**If you opt for a Portuguese escola primária your best route is
to visit a few near your residence and speak to the teachers
and head (diretor/a) and ask to be shown around. That will
give a clear indication of facilities, materials and activities,
and children's happiness/boredom levels.**

SECONDARY SCHOOLING

Portuguese
If you decide to send your child into the Portuguese sector, you can seek advice beforehand from the Ministry of
Education in Lisbon, at Gabinete Relações Internacionais, Avenida 5 de Outubro 35-37, 1000 Lisboa. You
can also get advice in the UK from the Portuguese Education Ministry official based at the Portuguese Consulate
General in London, which will gladly give you information on the Portuguese education system.

International
Alternatively, you may choose one of the international
schools, of which the following could be considered:

Oporto

◆ Oporto British School, Rua da Cerca 326/338, Foz do Douro, 4150 Porto. Tel: 22-616 6660. Fax: 22-616 6668. Email: obsintschl@mail.telepac.pt UK and International curriculum with good facilities. Well-established, ECIS member. Head of School: Mr Bob Carrington.

◆ CLIP – Colégio Luso-International do Porto, Esplanada Rio de Janeiro, Matosinhos, 4100-424 Porto. Tel: 22-610 0860. Fax: 22-610 2307. Email: clip@clip.pt English instruction, with UK/international curriculum. Headmaster: Ruben de Freitas Cabral.

◆ Michael Scott School (Oporto International School), Rua Duarte de Oliveira 283, Largo do Guimarães, Perosinho, 4415 Carvalhos. Tel: 22-764 1925. Small school, ages 4½ to 12, with a wide curriculum and instruction in English. Located outside Porto in country setting.

Lisbon

◆ American Christian International Academy, Av. de Sintra, Lote 1, 2750 Cascais. Tel: 21-486 1860. Fax: 21-485 1860. Email: orehotsky@aol.com US curriculum, small school, age range 5 to 14. Director: David Orehotsky.

◆ St Dominic's International School, Outeiro da Polima-Arneiro, 2775 São Domingos da Rana, Lisbon. Tel: 21-444 0434/4647/6092. Fax: 21-444 3072. Email: adm@dominic.mailpac.pt Dominican-run with English instruction. International curriculum with GNVQs in some subjects. Principal: Maria R Empis.

◆ St Julian's School, Quinta Nova, Carcavelos, 2777 Codex. Tel: 21-457 0140. Fax: 21-458 3729. Email: mail@stjulians.com British and International curriculum, with Common Entrance exam. Headmaster: F David Styan.

Algarve

◆ International School of the Algarve (Porches), Apartado 80, Porches, 8400 Lagoa, Algarve. Tel: 282-342547. Fax: 282-53787. Email: porches72@hotmail.com Large, purpose-built school with good facilities. English curriculum with a good Portuguese section as well. Headmaster: John Butterworth.

◆ Vilamoura International School, Apt 856, 8125-911 Vilamoura. Tel: 289-321585. Fax: 289-321388. Email: info@cl-int-vilamoura.ecis.pt Purpose-built, established school with Portuguese, English and international sections. Director: Renato Costa.

◆ Escola Internacional São Lourenço, Sitio Da Rabona, 8135 Almancil, Algarve. Tel: 289-398328. Fax: 289-398298. Email: eisl@mail.telepac.pt Small school, very friendly. English Curriculum. Headmistress: Jean Chinn.

Other institutions include smaller schools particularly dotted along the Algarve – be careful with some of these as they may display some, if not all, of the characteristics mentioned later in our case history. For addresses of additional schools in Portugal, see Useful Contacts at back of book.

FURTHER EDUCATION/TRAINING

As it is recognised that a large part of the Portuguese workforce is unskilled, efforts are now well under way to provide a more practical-orientated education and a wide range of training courses, usually through evening classes.

Polytechnics

Almost every district now boasts a polytechnic (**escola politécnica**), offering 3 year vocational courses in a wide range of subjects, from computer technology to the catering trade. Polytechnics are linked closely to industry, running sandwich courses similar to the UK, and to job centres (**institutos de emprego**), who in turn also favour industrial and business links. The job centres also run their own vocational courses. To apply for a place on one of these courses you can get advice from the Instituto do Emprego e Formação Profissional (IEFP), at Av. José Malhoa, 11, 1070 Lisboa. Tel: 21 7273123. Fax: 21 7265755.

Other institutes

There are also now many institutes opening up, with money pouring in from the EU, providing evening, and some daytime, courses in various subjects. The main option seems to be for training in practical computer skills (**informática**), but other choices include: secretarial studies, languages, management training (**gestão**), and accounts (**contabilidade**).

Be wary of private colleges offering 'Mickey Mouse' certificates, that is, a certificate to say you have completed a course with them that has no real qualification value when job searching. So do enquire as to standards and nationally recognised courses. In the UK you can get information from The Comparability Co-ordinator, Employment Department, Qualifications and Standards Branch, QSI, Room E454, Moorfoot, Sheffield S1 4PQ.

Courses at polytechnics tend to be reasonably priced. Private courses can be much more, so shop around.

UNIVERSITY COURSES
Until recently it was difficult to be accepted on a Portuguese university course; usually you were required to already be the holder of a university degree, and in some cases you had to have a Masters degree even to be accepted on a first degree course. For those studying Portuguese at an English university it was possible to spend a year at university in Portugal, but only on a specific language course, and as part of your integrated study programme in the UK. The situation is easing now, but a basic requirement for acceptance will almost always include proficiency in the language.

University education is very cheap, consequently there are many students clamouring for few places. Private universities exist but are expensive in comparison. University education has seen much unrest in recent years, through lack of facilities, overcrowding and lack of tutor interest (tutors can earn a lot more in the lucrative private sector). A recent example involved law students at Coimbra who were up in arms because a lecture hall with only 40 seats was provided for a lecture for 400 students. Another great problem, according to Carlos Furtado, of Coimbra University, is that students are not adequately prepared at school for academic life at a higher level, and many fail at university. It's not surprising that most Portuguese academics or professional people took higher degrees abroad. Money is now being invested in higher education to improve matters all round.

If you are interested in pursuing a course in Portugal, contact the institutions listed previously under Polytechnics and then make contact with a department at one of the universities. For enquiries about grants contact in the first instance the Portuguese Embassy in London.

LANGUAGE COURSES

In the UK
If you want to start your language learning before you leave the UK, contact your local College of Further Education, or Adult Education department of a university, who will inform you of any course in your area. Portuguese studies are not widely available, and where they are, they are usually beginners' courses, ranging from 5 week survival courses to 20 week basic studies. The BBC produced a summary of courses available. You can obtain a copy by writing to the address in the Useful Contacts list. There may also be small, private tutorial groups functioning. Should you experience any difficulty in locating a suitable course near you, please contact me c/o How To Books and I'll see if I can help.

In Portugal

Once in Portugal there is a wide range of language courses available. The universities, particularly in Lisbon, Coimbra and Oporto, run a summer course, and longer courses (6-12 months), for serious students; usually the course will cover a lot of grammar rather than get-by type studies. They are excellent courses; usually the class will be a mixture of nationalities so it's a great way to make friends.

These courses do take up considerable time, so if you're looking for something part-time you should enrol at one of the numerous private language colleges or schools. A scan through the *Yellow Pages* of your town will throw up a variety of them. It's a good idea to check out the credentials of potential teachers before you register, as often people are employed to teach their own language, without any understanding of a language-learner's requirements. The British Council in Lisbon can help you with addresses, and standard names such as the Berlitz/Eurolingua/Interlingua schools should offer the quality tuition you need. There is always a registration fee (**matrícula**) as well as course fees. Further addresses in Useful Contacts list.

INTERNATIONAL STUDENT EXCHANGES

Student exchanges have been working very successfully with students worldwide each year visiting new cultures, studying a new language, learning to get on with people from different nations and broadening their personal and career horizons. If you are a university student and you are interested in spending some time in Portugal (apart from the language courses already mentioned), the main organisations are:

Erasmus Grants available to cover travel and living expenses – students are supposed to be exempt from registration and tuition fees. The award is for students who would like to carry out a formally recognised part of their course in any EU country. Further information from your own university or from UK Erasmus Students Grants Council, The University of Kent, Canterbury CT2 7PD. Grants are also available for staff and university departments.

Lingua Programmes specially for language learning measures. Information available from Lingua, 2-3 place du Luxembourg, B-1040 Brussels, or in the UK from Central Bureau, 10 Spring Gardens, London SW1A 2BN. Tel: (020) 7389 4004. Fax: (020) 7389 4426. Website: http:// www/britcoun.org

Science Plan For researchers and science students. Information from Stimulation Action, DG XII-H-1, Commission of the European Communities, 200 rue de la loi, B-1049 Brussels.

Other schemes are also functioning – contact the London office of the Commission of European Communities, 8 Storeys Gate, London SW1P 3AT for the *Guide to the European Community programmes in the fields of education, training and youth.*

Youth for Europe Grants available for youth groups and their leaders – information available from Youth Exchange

Centre, The British Council. The centre also produces a handy booklet on Portugal, with useful addresses of youth and voluntary groups.

A WORD OF WARNING: CASE HISTORY

Mr and Mrs G, after some years in education in the UK, decided to move to Portugal and open their own school. Initially their grandiose plans included setting up a 'University of the Algarve'; reality proved to be very different. The school they set up worked from two apartments in a small town near Lagoa. Mr G, a very smooth talker, persuaded a handful of parents to enrol their children as pupils, with great promises of educational and cultural opportunities. A convincing prospectus was available, and it was easy to be impressed by Mr G's enthusiasm for his creation. However, an exposé of the school revealed:

◆ Misleading information in the prospectus, including the range of subjects available, school facilities – the library, for instance, consisted of a few shelves in a locked box room and the science lab was in fact a kitchen.

◆ Untrained and unqualified teachers – whereas 6th form colleges and adult education do not require teaching degrees, British mainstream schools insist on a BEd or PGCE from their staff.

◆ Low staff morale, problems with pay, tax and insurance, and even work permit doubts (although that at least is not applicable now), resulting in high staff turnover.

- Incorrect preparation for exams, and to the horror of many, exam papers were found accessible to anyone, instead of being locked away.

- Students' attitudes very lapse – some would turn up late or even fall asleep in class due to late nights at clubs.

The list is endless. The school was investigated by official bodies, and eventually the staff took over the running of the establishment. And what of Mr and Mrs G? Perhaps licking their wounds... or perhaps running an international school near you...

CHECKLIST

1. Have you considered what type of schooling is appropriate for your children?

2. What do you know about the educational institutions where you plan on living?

3. Have you requested prospectuses and arranged a visit?

4. Can you afford school fees, if not what will you do?

5. Have you checked out a few language schools to compare what language courses are on offer?

6. Have you investigated the situation for student/teacher exchanges, and possible funding?

(11)

Health Services

BEFORE YOU LEAVE

If you know in advance that your stay will be a long one, it is advisable to see your doctor for a general check-up. You should also take the following actions:

- Now is the time to have tetanus injections, and to ensure that any young children going with you have had any routine vaccinations they require. For Portugal you will not require any further injections.

- Check with your doctor if you take a prescribed medicine regularly – if he/she can prescribe a bulk supply for you to take with you (this is also helpful for those taking the Pill), and what is its, or its equivalent, availability in Portugal, should you run out.

- If you have any potentially serious condition, a doctor's letter or certificate would be useful although you may be charged a small fee for it.

- A dental check-up before you go is also recommended, as treatment in Portugal is expensive (see Dentist section).

- Make a note of addresses and phone numbers of your own doctor, dentist/local clinic in case you need to contact them whilst you are away.

- Prepare a small first aid kit to take with you, with basic necessities such as bandages, plasters, cream, insect repellent, aspirin. It needn't take up much space, and it at least makes you prepared for minor problems.

- UK sickness benefit holders should contact their local DSS to enquire about receiving payment whilst away.

- The Post Office has copies of the handy leaflet *Health advice for travellers* (T6). Leaflet T6 also contains the application forms for the famous E111 – the form which enables you to receive emergency treatment in the EU. This needs to be filled in and stamped by the Post Office. Keep a photocopy for reference.

OBTAINING INSURANCE

Form E111 (see example in Figure 18)

This form, as mentioned previously, entitles members of EU states to seek medical attention whilst travelling abroad. The form, which covers yourself and any members of your family travelling with you, is authorised at the Post Office, and is valid permanently, so you must keep it safe. However, it is only valid for short trips abroad, whilst you keep UK residency. It also only applies to emergency treatment and medication, and not general health care.

If you should need urgent treatment, you should show your passport to the hospital concerned and ask to be treated under the EU arrangements. Although treatment under the state scheme is free, any further X-rays, checkups and tests must be paid for, but you can usually claim a refund by taking the original document to the local sickness insurance body (information from the **centro de saúde** – health centre). If you return to the UK without reclaiming costs, you may send receipts and your E111 to the Overseas branch of the DSS, but this is a long process. Remember, the E111 is only for emergency treatment and should only be used for short stay situations. Students studying or on a work experience visit require form **E138**, from the DSS, International Services section of the Contributions Agency (see Useful Contacts).

Portuguese state insurance (NI/caixa)
If you are working in Portugal, your employer should be deducting your contributions to the health system, so entitling you to free state assistance. Some treatment and medication, such as doctors' consultations, still have to be paid for, but can be set off against tax, so do keep all receipts.

Private schemes
For short stays, check whether holiday insurance covers you for certain treatments. Many people also take out a private insurance cover, either personally, through companies like BUPA or PPP, or collectively as a group at work. If you are a resident but not working (therefore not paying caixa) you may well have difficulties being treated in the state system, and are advised to arrange private insurance. Pensioners are looked after.

Useful leaflets	Form T6 health advice	Available from Post Office
	Working in Portugal	Available from Employment office

See 'Instructions' overleaf

| E 111 | GB | (1)

CERTIFICATE OF ENTITLEMENT TO BENEFITS IN KIND DURING A STAY IN A MEMBER STATE

Reg. 1408/71: Art. 22.1.a.i; Art. 22.3; Art. 31.a
Reg. 574/72: Art. 20.4; Art. 21.1; Art. 23; Art. 31.1 and 3

1

☐ Employed person   ☐ Pensioner (scheme for employed persons)   ☐ Other

☐ Self-employed person   ☐ Pensioner (scheme for self-employed persons)

(Surname (¹ᵃ), Previous names (¹ᵃ), D.N.I. (²ᵃ), address (²))

Postcode

1.1 Identification No (²ᵇ) .... Date of birth ....

1.2 ☐ The person named above is covered by a scheme for self-employed persons as referred to in Annex 11 to Regulation 574/72

2   Members of the family (³)

2.1 Surname (¹ᵃ)	Forenames	Previous names	Date of birth	Identification No (²ᵇ)
....	....	....	....	....
....	....	....	....	....
....	....	....	....	....
....	....	....	....	....

Fig. 18. Emergency treatment form E111.

180

2.2 Permanent address (²) (⁴)

3 The above-named persons are entitled to benefits in kind under sickness and maternity insurance.

These benefits may be provided

3.1 (⁵) ☐ from .... to .... inclusive

3.2 (⁵) ☐ from ....

---

4 Competent institution

4.1 Name — DEPARTMENT OF SOCIAL SECURITY,   Code number (⁶) ....

4.2 Address (²) — CONTRIBUTIONS AGENCY, OVERSEAS CONTRIBUTIONS,
.... NEWCASTLE UPON TYNE, UK NE98 1YX

4.3 Stamp

4.4 Date ....
4.5 Signature

4.6 Valid from .... to ....

4.7 Stamp   4.8 Date ....

4.9 Signature

4.10 Valid from .... to ....

4.11 Stamp   4.12 Date ....

4.13 Signature

---

5 Competent French institution for non-occupational accidents sustained by self-employed farmers

5.1 Name ....   Code number (⁶) ....

5.2 Address (²) ....

5.3 Stamp

5.4 Date ....
5.5 Signature

THE PORTUGUESE HEALTH SYSTEM

The health system is run by the **Ministério de Saúde**, through a series of local centres, administrative (**administração regional de saúde**), and the health centres (**centros de saúde**). Treatment in a hospital, within the state system is free, as is vital medication, whereas treatment in a centro de saúde is not. If your illness is not serious it's surprising how much the local chemists are used for consultation (free!).

The Portuguese health system has been criticised for its lack of facilities, lengthy waiting times and lack of care and attention. A recent, disturbing, report stated that Portuguese hospitals are not capable of detecting the human variant of BSE ('mad cow disease'). Although no cases have ever been reported in Portugal, it is telling that a whole system has come under fire in this way. Despite various reforms the modernisation process takes time, and apart from the larger, industrialised cities such as Lisbon and Oporto, most local hospitals are small and many are outdated. Some towns only have a centro de saúde, which cannot cover every kind of treatment, so transfer to the nearest hospital is a common occurrence. Portuguese doctors, nurses and dentists are dedicated, qualified professionals; it is their situation which sometimes lets them down.

State or private – how to choose

One hears both good and bad stories about the state system, but you must consider the situation in view of your own circumstances.

- Can you afford an extra, private insurance cover?

- Would you be entitled to care in the UK (are you keeping UK residence)?

- Do you have a condition which may need long-term treatment? If so, how can it be funded?

- Does holiday insurance cover you in the short term for your requirements?

PRIVATE CLINICS

There are private clinics, especially in the more densely-populated tourist areas and around the Algarve in particular. Private centres are usually advertised in the *Yellow Pages* (look under centros de saúde/clínicas privadas). Foreign-run centres also advertise in the English publications, and offer a range of services. You can ring to make an initial appointment, but check from the outset if a charge is made for consultation – usually there is. You may feel happier paying a bit extra for the comfort of being able to communicate a little more easily with the doctor, especially if your ailment is complicated, or of a more personal nature.

There is a British hospital in Lisbon, at Rua Saraiva de Carvalho, 49. Tel: 21 395 5067. All the staff speak English. For treatment in private centres you will be expected to meet the cost of all assistance personally, with no agreements available for refunds, so most people would need private insurance cover for this type of treatment.

See addresses in Useful Contact list for private clinics, including those offering alternative medical approaches, such as homeopathy.

THE DOCTOR

You may register with any doctor, Portuguese or otherwise. All services have to be paid for, even consultations, so if you have hypochondriac tendencies, make sure you also have a full purse! Remember to keep all medical receipts for tax purposes.

CHEMISTS

The chemist's shop (**a farmácia**) can be a fascinating old fashioned place; step into one and you step back in time to the traditional wooden counter, glass fronted cabinets on the walls, many filled with exciting looking glass bottles, and dark recesses into the back of the premises, from where appear white-coated assistants bearing lotions and potions to cure your ailment. It all rather smacks of a Dickensian apothecary. Modern chemists also now exist in abundance, in light, pristine shops. All chemists are invaluable places to seek help.

Opening times

From 9 am to 1 pm and 3 pm–7 pm, Monday–Friday and on Saturdays, mornings only. Most towns have at least two or three farmácias, one of which will stand by for emergencies (**de serviço**). If you need a chemist on a Sunday for example, there will usually be a sign in the farmácia window, informing which one will be open and at what times. The local press also contain this information. But don't be surprised if even the emergency chemist keeps you waiting – I once needed some migraine tablets and had to wait over an hour for the chemist to open up, despite the emergency time displayed in the window. By that time I needed almost the whole packet!

Availability of medicines

The pharmacists are very knowledgeable, and will usually find something to alleviate your problem. Some medication available easily in the UK cannot be found, though, so if you run out, take the empty bottle or packet so that they can match it with an equivalent. Headache tablets are not on sale in supermarkets, as they are in the UK; you must buy them from the chemist.

Useful expressions

Tem algo para. . .	enxaquecas	migraines
	dor de cabeça	headache
	dor de estômago	stomache-ache
	insolação	sunstroke

$\Big\}$?

(Do you have something for...?)

See also Glossary of Useful Phrases

DENTISTS

Dental charges are (like telephone bills) notoriously high. Whether you register with a Portuguese or a foreign dentist makes no difference, although you may find that some Portuguese dentists prefer proof of residence-status, despite the fact that EU reciprocal arrangements now allow for emergency treatment anywhere within the EU. A flick through the *Yellow Pages* will give you some addresses; foreign dentists also tend to advertise in the English journals such as *Algarve Resident* and *APN*, and again, asking around will give you some indication of recommended surgeries.

If you just want to register, then take your documents, explain your situation, saying that you would like to be on the register for future treatment.

If you find yourself in need of treatment, go along and ask for an appointment as soon as possible – it may be better to ring round a few first to see who can fit you in. Do be warned – however professional and charming the dentist may appear, his behaviour may mask the thought of money rolling in. Be careful not to agree to any treatment you don't need urgently, such as polishing and cleaning, or your bill will rise steeply, and you may even be told to come back to get the original treatment next time. (This happened to a few people I know with a dentist in the Algarve.) Prices are often at a fixed hourly rate so the longer the dentist keeps you chatting the better (for him). You will also be charged for an initial check up.

Dental treatment costs can be deducted against tax, so keep all your receipts.

Many people decide to keep their own UK dentist and visit him/her whenever they are home, particularly if they need extensive treatment. Unfortunately there will always be the odd occasion when urgent attention is needed – keep smiling as you write the cheque!

ACCIDENT PROCEDURES

If you are involved in an accident, or are at the scene of one, be it transport, domestic or assault, remember more than anything to keep calm. Try to follow these simple steps:

♦ Get someone to call an ambulance (**ambulância**),or if you have to do it yourself dial 112 free. This is the national emergency number, and gives you access to all three emergency services. It operates in English, French and Portuguese. Try to give the location as accurately as possible – name of town/city centre or outside/street names/nearby shops.

♦ Make sure the victims are as comfortable as possible, but do not move them as this may cause further injury.

♦ Keep talking to them reassuring that help is on its way.

♦ If there is risk of fire, request the fire brigade (**bombeiros**) on 112.

♦ If it is a transport accident, do not move any vehicle until the police arrive.

If the accident is within a town you will find people rally round to help, phoning and informing doctors, but if you are out of town you may need to flag down a car or run to the nearest house/farm/bar. Once the ambulance has arrived, you may accompany the victim to hospital. Depending on the seriousness of the accident, you should not expect to get seen immediately. One of my students was knocked off a moped, and although her injuries were quite minimal, she was kept waiting in a long corridor, half naked, with bloodied bodies all around. Treatment is not as super efficient as in the BBC's *Casualty*.

After the ordeal there comes the aftermath, the paperwork, almost as painful as the initial injuries. If you have been a witness there will no doubt be police enquiries to fulfill; otherwise the hospital register will have to be filled in with the victim's details, address and circumstances. It's a good idea to have copies of your documents with you. Another good idea is to study a first aid handbook before you go abroad.

PREGNANCY

If you are pregnant at the time you move to Portugal you should ask your own GP's advice about on-going personal healthcare, and check with your local health authority about receiving benefits related to maternity. If you are on any special medication for your condition, ensure you have a plentiful supply, or ask your doctor for the generic names for the items so you easily find them in Portugal. You may need Form E112 . This will entitle you to free or reduced-cost treatment. To obtain this you must send a copy of your E111, plus a letter from your GP or midwife, stating your expected date of confinement, to the Department of Health, International Branch, Room 512, Richmond House, 79 Whitehall, London SW1A 2NS. Tel: (020) 7210 5318. Try to do this in plenty of time before you expect to leave the UK. You will be informed of your entitlements within Portugal.

Once in Portugal, or should you fall pregnant whilst living there, your doctor there will give you all the guidance you would normally receive back home, informing you of your options for treatment (private or state), plus helping you through the physical aspects of your pregnancy. In Portugal you have access to an abundance of fresh, cheap vegetables, fruit and fish products, which will contribute to a healthy pregnancy for you and your baby.

Registering the birth

You need to register your baby's birth within 30 days. The hospital will give you a document confirming the birth, the sex of the child, the date, plus that you are the mother. At this stage you do not need a name for your child. The Portuguese name list for new-born children contains very few names of non-Portuguese origin. This means that should you wish to give your child a name with a different spelling, you must first request a letter from the British Embassy which states the nationality of the two parents, and that the chosen name(s) for the child are acceptable names in the UK. The baby can then be registered at the Conservatório do Registo Civil in the district where the baby was born. You will need the following documents:

- hospital confirmation document
- letter from your Embassy concerning choice of name
- your birth certificate and that of your partner
- marriage certificate (if applicable)
- your passports.

You will receive a birth certificate for the child (**Boletim de Nascimento**). You must apply to the Embassy or Consulate for a country of origin passport for the child, and you may be asked to register the birth there to receive UK citizenship for the child. Children born in Portugal to non-Portuguese parents who have resided there for at least six years, and who work for a Portuguese company may claim Portuguese nationality when they reach majority.

Maternity benefits

If you have been working, and paying into the Social

Security System, you will be entitled to maternity benefits. You must have been in paid employment for at least six months prior to claiming benefit. Maternity allowance is paid for 90 days, and is claimed from your regional social security centre - you will be asked to provide evidence of your situation (work details, birth certificate or letter from health centre). Paternity allowance is also available. For further guidance whilst in Portugal, ask at your nearest health centre, or check with Consular staff for advice.

DISABILITIES

Facilities for the disabled are still very limited in Portugal, although some new buildings are now providing access for wheelchairs. There is some availability of reserved parking, and an increase in access to toilet facilities. Facilities are by no means widespread, and you would be advised to check carefully in advance if you need specific help.

Health centres and clinics should be able to give you details of local support groups, and organisations within the ex-pat community do a lot of work in this respect. One such example is the Mira Sintra Social, Leisure, Rehabilitation Centre and Gymnasium for the handicapped, in the Lisbon area. More information on the project can be obtained via the Anglo-Portuguese Society (see Useful Contacts).

CLIMATIC CONDITIONS

As with many trips abroad, be it brief visits or longer stays, there will always be an element of surprise, which could turn into shock, where the weather is concerned. The climate in Portugal is, on the whole, an agreeable one for most people, yet year after year stories come to light of visitors not taking precautions (for heat and cold) and ruining their stay. If you know you have a health condition which is affected by extremes in weather, then go prepared for anything.

Heat

The summer months, from May until September, but particularly June, July and August, can cause unnecessary suffering when visitors do not take heed of strong warnings about the harmful effects of the sun. We all know by now that over exposure to the sun will lead to forms of skin cancer, so it doesn't make sense to lie on a beach in the blistering heat all day, yet how many people still do it? The Portuguese, on the other hand, although lovers of beach trips, are wise to the sun's unrelenting rays and visit the beach in the early morning and again at the end of the afternoon, usually taking a large sunshade. Children in particular should be well covered up as their young skin will be an easy target.

Apart from sunstroke and related sun ailments, the heat itself can be very overbearing. As temperatures soar into the 100s (°F) you must learn to slow down to a more leisurely pace. Learn to get through work in the mornings and don't expect too much from yourself in the afternoon. Stroll, don't stride out, and always carry plenty of water on any journey – you'll certainly need it. Dress cool, act cool and think cool and you will survive it.

Cold

Surprisingly to most people, the winters may not be as full of warmth and sunshine as is described in many travel brochures. Northern Portugal has a winter climate very much like the UK, with rain and snow up in the hills. In places like the flat plains of the Alentejo, unprotected from the elements, temperatures drop incredibly and freezing conditions are to be expected. I once spent a Christmas under five blankets, with socks, gloves, balaclava in the Alentejo, and yet the days were sunny with blue skies.

Even the Algarve is affected – from January to early March the heavens can open with a constant downpour of miserable water. Combined with lack of adequate heating in property, this can lead to a cold, damp time, with all the associated discomforts. Make sure you are armed with adequate warm clothing, waterproofs, suitable wet weather footwear (there is nothing worse than damp feet), and facilities for getting warm where you are staying.

PRECAUTIONS

There are many ways in which you can help yourselves, either before you leave the UK, or having arrived in Portugal. If you are prone to cold-like illnesses, maybe you should consider a flu jab, and although Portugal is not really a danger zone for tropical diseases, you may feel reassured by asking your doctor for advice on immunisation against malaria or hepatitis. The hot months also bring the tiresome insects such as mosquitoes, and despite protestations that those in the Mediterranean do not carry disease, you really cannot be sure nowadays, so check with your local doctor or hospital before departing. Arm yourselves with insect repellent as the wonderful warm nights are easily spoilt by hungry insects clamouring for a taste of foreign blood. Cover up if you can. A plug-in device can be bought to keep them away from you indoors, but follow instructions properly, some of the substances emitted can be dangerous within a confined space.

Another horror spoken little of, yet potentially very dangerous, is tick fever. In the warm, damp early Spring months, small ticks abound in the countryside and are easily transmitted to animals roaming in the grass. They attach themselves to the creatures' body, feeding off their blood, and ballooning up into quite a repellent-looking blob. Not only do they sap the energy out of the animal, but you should be very careful not to touch these parasites at this stage, as they can transfer to you, and if bitten by them, a form of meningitis can occur, with symptoms such as hallucinations. If your own animal picks these up, either rip them off quickly with a comb, or tweezers, or try burning them off with a match (carefully). Vets can also recommend powders.

Personal cleanliness is also important, so daily showers are vital if possible.

Most ailments can be cured with medication, but it's wise to be sensible in your movements and behaviour, and, although perhaps stating the obvious, take all necessary precautions if you are intending to have a sexual relationship with anyone.

CHECKLIST
1. Have you visited your doctor/dentist/optician before you depart, and do you have all your instructions for medication?

2. Do you have an E111/E112/E128, or private health insurance?

3. Have you budgeted for medical fees?

4. Are you clear about emergency procedures?

5. Do you have the necessary information for claiming maternity benefits and registering your child's birth?

6. Are you well prepared for weather conditions?

(12)

Leisure and Travel

SOCIALISING AND ENTERTAINING
Whether you have gone to Portugal for business reasons, to study, or retire, part of your time there will be devoted to relaxing. A wide choice of activities abound, catering for all tastes, but a lot depends on where you live and your decision to either join in the Portuguese way of life, or to stick firmly to ex-pat communities.

Portuguese style
You will find that the Portuguese way of relaxing has its limitations: for example, in the UK you may be used to meeting people in a variety of social circles, such as at leisure centres, evening classes, church meetings, and craft displays; the Portuguese tend to concentrate their socialising around the bar or café. Often the whole family goes out in the evening and meets up with friends in the town square, to have a couple of drinks together. It is a common sight to see very young children running around playing together as late as 11 o'clock in the evening, as their parents sit and chat. In larger towns some people may visit their local swimming pool/tennis courts/gym, and aerobics is popular with the ladies and students. Little entertaining is done in the home, as the Portuguese often fear their modest lifestyle may not reach your standard.

However, should you be invited to dinner, expect to be treated lavishly.

Ex-pat style

As an ex-pat you may wish to confine yourself to activities organised by your community, but the danger is always that you will perpetuate the myth of the insular group of people who are often construed as the typical British ex-pat, with no links whatsoever with their host society. There is no truer saying than 'when in Rome...', and besides, many a business deal, many a firm friendship, many a best-selling book is clinched over a couple of drinks at an inviting and unrushed bar.

SOCIAL EVENTS – BIRTHS, WEDDINGS, DEATHS

Births

It is customary to send a card on the birth of a child to people you know. If they are close friends you may wish to offer a gift to the mother and/or child. The baptism of a child is generally a cause for great celebration, but usually only family and close friends are invited. If you do receive an invitation, dress well and take along a present.

Weddings

If you are invited to a Portuguese wedding, respond immediately, stating whether you will be attending or not. Usually presents can be sent to the bride up to the day of the wedding; if it is a lavish affair the bride may have registered with certain high-class gift shops which will wrap and deliver a present on your behalf. If the event is to be more modest you can take the present with you. Ask beforehand to check procedures.

You may be invited to the ceremony (in the case of a church wedding), or reception (**copo d'água**). If you are going along to the church, people tend to arrive early and chat outside. Not many churches have adequate parking nearby (many are in town centres), so ensure you have enough time to find a space if necessary. Invitations will usually state what dress code is required. It's important to get that right.

After the ceremony it is customary to find the newlyweds and entourage driving round and round the town centre pipping car horns; a typical Saturday afternoon occurrence.

Deaths

If you should be in a position (personally or through close friends) where a funeral takes place, remember that the dead are normally buried within 24 hours in Portugal. You can offer condolences at the family residence, or chapel of rest. Unless you knew the deceased well you should not approach the open coffin. If you accompany the cortège to the cemetery you will find a difference from UK burials. As the coffin is lowered into the ground it is opened up again for lime to be thrown into it.

Flowers and cards of condolence are appropriate to send. There will usually also be a seventh day mass for the deceased. Mourning traditionally lasted a year, but now can be as short as three months. However, some widows still maintain the old way of wearing black for the rest of their life.

PUBS AND CLUBS

Again the choice between Portuguese and foreign-run location is yours, and none more so than in the Algarve, the increasing enclave of ex-pat residents.

Pubs

Most bars and pubs on the coasts are British/foreign owned, and the prices reflect it. Unfortunately the reputation of certain groups of visitors to places like the Algarve and the Spanish costas has tarnished the image of these drinking holes, and tragically the image is often lived up to. If a plate of sausage and chips and a pint of Carlsberg is your idea of enjoying yourself abroad, fine, the choice of location is endless – just follow your nose and the myriad of English pub signs. If you prefer to integrate more into Portuguese life, travel inland a few miles, and look for a locally patronised bar, with Portuguese prices and hospitality. Don't be concerned if you are viewed with curiosity for a while, if you can order your drinks in Portuguese and exchange a few words you'll quickly be accepted.

Clubs

Drinks in clubs tend to be far more expensive, so do be cautious. Some clubs have an entrance fee, often including a drink; however, many can be entered with more ease if you know the bouncer/waiter/owner! Be careful in places where you are given a 'tab' for the evening, where drinks are just noted on your ticket until you want to leave and you are faced with the consequences of having got carried way with your drinking. Clubs in places like Oporto and Lisbon are packed out from Thursday – Saturday, and become unbearably hot and sticky, especially in the summer months. Opening times are much later than in the UK, from about 10 pm – 4 or 5 am. Nightspots in Lisbon are now the in place for the Iberian fashion-concious.

Smaller towns have a much smaller choice of venue, but most dance fanatics should be able to find at least one place. The country towns also hold frequent village dances, with a local band playing, which can be great fun.

SPORTS

As mentioned at the beginning of this chapter, sport does play its role in socialising, especially amongst the younger age groups, but by no means exclusively so. In some places, the Algarve in particular, private leisure clubs are available, but membership is usually quite high and again you are likely to encounter mostly ex-pats there. For more details on sports see Regional Directory and Useful Contacts.

Golf

The ideal destination for golf enthusiasts, with an ever-growing choice of courses, and not only in the south. Portugal aims to create more courses over the next few years, which will make it one of the prime choices for good golf play in the world. Some of the recommended courses include Pine Cliffs, Alto Golf, Penina, and Vilamoura. For a more comprehensive list, with full details of fees, contact the Portuguese Golf Federation (see Useful Contacts).

Football

The Portuguese are fanatical about their football, the two leading opposing teams being Benfica and Sporting FC. On Sunday afternoons it is not unusual to encounter dozens of men ambling around listening to the big match on their pocket radios. I once came across a beautiful park with an ornate bandstand in the middle of Évora, and sat down to take in the tranquillity of the afternoon, only to be shocked into reality by a loudspeaker booming out the live broadcast of a popular match.

Tennis

This tends to be situated around private clubs, and mostly in larger cities, but many schools have a tennis court marked out on a gravel pitch, and there are usually no objections to usage at a weekend.

Swimming

Easily accessible as most towns have a pool (**piscina municipal**), pay as you enter. Many insist you have a bathing hat (**uma toca**) and should you arrive without one, you will be asked to buy one before entering the pool. Swimming in the seas is practised, of course, but take care as not only are some beaches rather polluted, but some parts of the coast are particularly dangerous, such as the long stretch at Caparica, south across the river from Lisbon.

Windsurfing

Probably *the* in-sport amongst young people, with excellent waves in the Algarve, and up on the coast from Lisbon – Praia das maçãs, Guincho...

Horse riding

Facilities mainly in the South.

Slide/Splash

Waterparks are great fun for all the family; there are some on the south coast and near Lisbon.

Bullfighting

Not as popular as in Spain, but still considered 'sport' and 'entertainment'. As in Spain, tickets are priced according not only to where you sit, but also depend on how much sun you can bear. The prices range from **sol** seats (in the sun), to **sol e sombra** (seats where the sun will move off you half-way through) to **sombra** (in the shade). Bear this in mind on a hot, dusty Saturday afternoon, which is when most fights take place. Whatever anyone tells you that 'the bull is not killed in a Portuguese fight', do not kid yourself – the bull still suffers the same torture as in Spain, and is actually killed outside the ring afterwards, and is taken to the butchers. The major difference with the Spanish fights is that there is much more display on horseback, and another feature is the appearance of the **pegadores**, a group of young men who stand in a long line, the first one goading the bull into a charge, at which time all the group try to get on the bull's back at the same time. Apart from the flamboyance, the only excitement is when someone is injured. Go if you must, and see for yourself. An expensive afternoon out.

HOBBIES

There is no reason why your own favourite pastime cannot continue in Portugal. The climate there makes it particularly conducive to outdoor pursuits from gardening to hill-walking, and also painting (the southern, Mediterranean light is fantastic).

You may prefer indoor activities – flower-arranging, reading, dressmaking, and you should find access to all the resources you need to enjoy your hobby.

If you require more specialist shops – model railways, philately, coin-collecting, for example – you may encounter a few problems. There are a couple of things you can do:

◆ before you leave the UK, visit your own local supplier and enquire about mail-order, or see if they have details of overseas outlets
◆ look up your hobby in the *Yellow Pages* in your Portuguese area
◆ ask the local library if they have any contact details
◆ put a request in one of the English publications.

Some of the ex-pat organisations, such as the International Women in Portugal (in Lisbon), run sessions on various hobbies. See Regional Directory.

THE ARTS

Although we may not hear about Portuguese arts so much yet in the UK, there is a wealth of culture in this small country, and through the effort of organisations such as the **Calouste-Gulbenkian**, awareness of Portuguese artistes is eventually seeping through to an appreciative UK audience.

Art

The Gulbenkian museum of modern art in Lisbon is a mecca for modern enthusiasts, and it also hosts Gulbenkian's private collection of art from many ages – priceless in terms of artistic value. Gulbenkhian was a Turkish oil magnate who lived for many years in Portugal, and left a great fortune to further the arts. Lisbon (and Oporto) are also home to a wide range of art galleries.

Museums
Many, from prehistoric remains to exquisite carriages (**museu dos coches** in Lisbon), all over the country. Usually closed on a Monday. Ask at the Turismo for details.

Theatre/opera/ballet
Especially in Oporto and Lisbon. Some great productions in the splendid **teatros**, and many other larger towns have a representative arena for drama. The Centro Cultural de Belém, in Lisbon, is a popular venue for performances of various kinds.

Cinema
Nearly all towns have a cinema, however small. Particularly popular with younger people. Some up to date releases, and Portuguese productions. Very cheap. The Amoreiras complex in Lisbon boasts ten screens.

Music
Fado – in Lisbon particularly there are many fado houses, many cater just for tourists, try and get Portuguese friends to take you to the real thing at about 3 am to experience the Portuguese soul in flight. Coimbra fado is the music of the students, many of whom will serenade diners in restaurants.

Folklore (**ranchos folclóricos**) – folklore groups dress in traditional costume, with music, songs and dancing. Annual competition usually in the Algarve, draws a crowd from all over the country.

Guitarra portuguesa – as opposed to the Spanish guitar. Very peculiar to Portugal, great exponents of it being Carlos

Paredes and Pedro Caldeira Cabral. Often Carlos Paredes gives concerts in the UK. Worth catching a glimpse of.

Classical – some good quality up and coming youngsters. See ads in the Portuguese newspapers who promote the concerts.

Popular – touring Brazilian/Angolan/Cape Verdian singers, all of whom bring echoes of the former empire.

TRAVEL

By car

If you have access to your own transport, you should take every opportunity to find out more about this delightful country. The main road systems (**estradas**) are excellent, but be prepared to be overtaken at great speed. As many towns are not accessible by train and some only reached by bus with difficulty, a car driver really has an advantage, especially if you fancy visiting places off the beaten track. For serious drivers, maps are available, such as the Michelin guides and AA maps, and are easy enough to follow. As most towns possess at least one hotel and half a dozen bars, stopping off places pose no problems, and make travelling a lot easier. On the main estradas there are similar eating places to our own motorway cafés, except you have to grapple your way to the bar if there is a coachload in, and few serve main meals. Away from the busy estradas and city centres of jamming car horns, driving around exploring non-tourist areas can add a real bonus to your stay.

By bus

Bus and rail travel is rather primitive at times, but transport usually runs on time and efficiently, and can be extremely good fun and an attractive way to see a lot of the country.

Unless you live in a remote country village, your local buses will be frequent, and within the larger cities, cover almost every inch of the ground you may need to visit. You can pay as you get on, stating your destination, or you can buy a book of tickets which cover a certain value of journey. In Lisbon, for example, there is a system of **zonas**, where all journeys within a given zone will be worth one ticket, the next zone two tickets and so on. As you board you have to clip your tickets in a little machine – just watch the person in front of you. For extended use of buses a variety of passes are available which also give travel on trams and elevators, plus admission to certain venues. The same applies to the Underground (**metro**) in Lisbon and Oporto. Bus tickets and passes are available from little kiosks dotted around the city.

Longer bus/coach journeys leave from the bus station (**rodoviária nacional** or **terminal de camionagem**). You can buy tickets beforehand, but can usually only get singles. Travel is much cheaper than in the UK, and on longer trips a few brief stops are made at bus stations for loo/food. The express coaches (**camionetas**) thundering between the South, Lisbon, Oporto, Braga, are as streamlined as any in the UK, with hostess service on many. Night journeys are frequent.

By train

Most trains are impressive, huge, silver-coloured affairs, the steps of which are incredibly difficult to mount, so do get someone to help you if you have luggage. The network is still small at the moment, and lines to some of the country regions, especially the Alentejo, are scarce, making it rather difficult to reach an exact destination. The popular destinations of Lisbon, Oporto and Faro are adequately covered by a choice of ordinary or express trains, with an expanding range of modern, sleek vehicles. The express from the south to Lisbon takes about three hours and costs approximately £10. The new express link between Lisbon and Oporto is very similar. There is a train from the south to Lisbon which travels through the night, taking about seven hours – quite an adventure, but extremely tiring. Be prepared on approaching the Lisbon area from the south, to disembark and transfer to a ferry boat, which will take you to Lisbon proper; as yet there is still no direct link across the river by train. Equally so, travelling southwards from Lisbon, your first transport will be from the Terreiro do Paço fluvial station at Lisboa riverside.

By cycle

Cycling is a great way to tour Portugal, but potentially also a dangerous one! Remember that Portuguese roads and drivers can make life on the move hazardous, unless you choose your routes with caution and cycle at unsociable hours. Refer to Chapter 9 for more details. You may be viewed with an air of bemusement in smaller villages, as this is a rare form of transport in Portugal. Cars may honk at you in good-natured acknowledgement.

HOLIDAYS

Visiting the North

The North has traditionally been the most conservative, religious, and, industrially, the most prosperous region in Portugal. The domain of the verdant vineyards and home to some of the most historically important towns and areas of outstanding beauty, it is truly a part of the country worth taking time to discover.

Oporto

Oporto is the capital city of these lands, where for centuries the time-honoured link with its oldest ally, England, has given rise to its thriving port wine industry. A trip along the riverbank at Vila Nova de Gaia, the southern bank of the river, will illuminate exactly to what extent the wine industry plays a part in life here. Most port wine houses or **fábricas** will offer a tour and sample tasting, whilst outside on the river you can still see some of the original old boats, the **rabões** or **barcos rabelos** which traditionally ferried the barrels along the river. Oporto is a busy city, with many UK business interests, particularly in the wood and textiles industries. Whilst here, try the local speciality, tripe (**tripas**). The people here are known as **os tripeiros** (tripe-sellers).

Coimbra

Coimbra, although smaller, is a trip back in time, as the old university here is very reminiscent of Oxford and Cambridge, and the students fly around in their gowns, especially at the time of their famous ceremony, **queima das fitas** – burning of ribbons on gowns. Also the fado in Coimbra is sung by young male students, often serenading under windows, and often to gain money for their studies.

Other places to visit

Braga – historical ecclesiastic city – first bishopric of Portugal, with very beautiful buildings.

Parque Nacional de Peneda-Gerês – wide expanse of protected land.

Serra da Estrela – mountainous region with popular ski resort in winter. Famous also for its cheese (queijo da serra).

Trás-os-Montes – region 'back of beyond' (literally beyond the hills), some parts like medieval Europe, granite-built basic cottages, few amenities, poor but very respected.

Ponte de Lima – very north, old market place, where they sell everything from livestock to whisky vats; also from jeans to plastic bowls.

Visiting Lisbon

Lisbon (**Lisboa**) is an exciting, cosmopolitan city with something for absolutely everyone. From vibrating night-life, to a rich cultural and arts scene; from a wide range of outdoor cafés from where to watch the bustle go by, to a myriad of fascinating areas to explore. A cooling breeze always makes its way up from the river Tejo and is very welcome in the summer months, when temperatures can soar to the 90s (°F). The Tejo is always afloat with busy ferry boats, and these provide a means of passing time, by crossing to various points over the river, or taking a longer boat trip up and down the estuary. The castle (**de São Jorge**) provides a wonderful vantage point from which to survey all of the city, and you can observe the interesting mix of old and new, as modern structures emerge from amid centuries-old mansions and elegant parks.

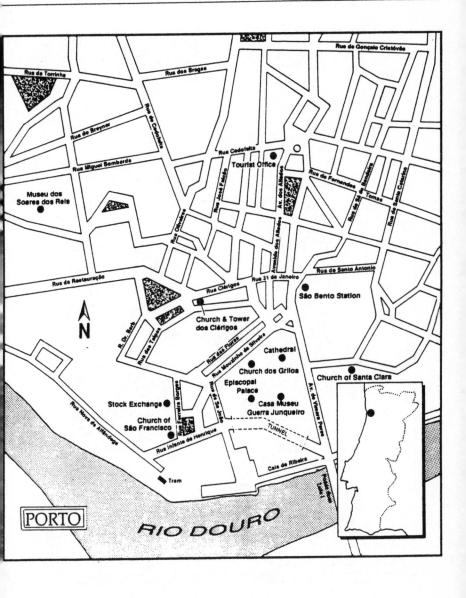

Fig. 19. Map of Central Porto.

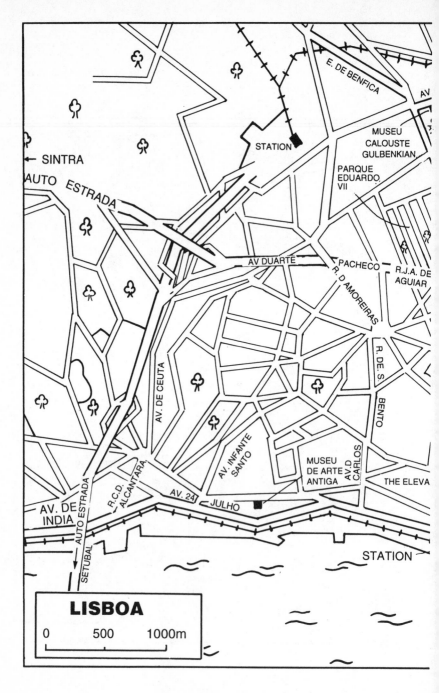

Fig. 20. Map of central Lisbon.

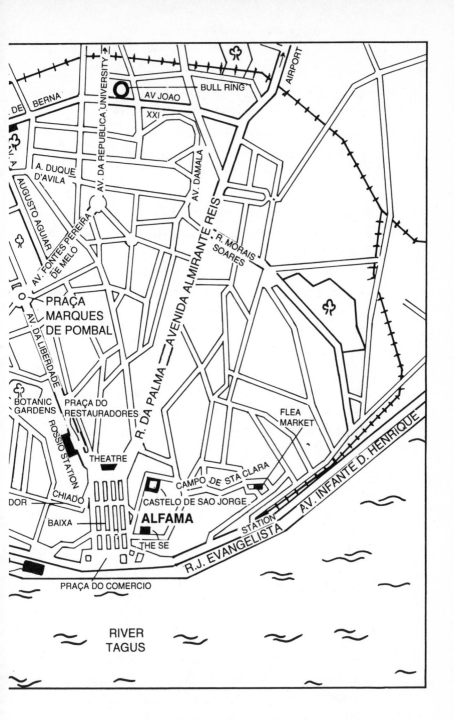

As in any major city, be careful with your valuables – some of the narrow cobbled streets in the Alfama area near the castle, and the Bairro Alto (home of most of the Fado houses) form real mazes and not everyone is to be trusted. Be sensible.

One place not to be missed is the almost world renowned eating place **Cervejaria de Trindade**, in the Bairro Alto, which is at its fullest after 10 pm each night. Famed for its steak and seafood, it's an ideal place to eat, and with prices at about £12 for two people to gorge themselves, including wine, you'll agree it's worth a visit.

Out and about from Lisbon why not take the train from Sodré station along the coast to what were once the elegant summer destinations of many European aristocrats, Cascais and Estoril? Sadly, much of their former glory has faded with the onslaught of the tourist boom, but they are still worth a visit.

Sintra is not far, with its palaces, castle and fairy tale town, a beautiful day out. If you can't face the tortuous climb to Pena palace, the way to travel is by taxi, or horse and carriage.

Visiting the South

The Alentejo
The area from Lisbon southwards is mostly taken up by the rolling plains of the Alentejo. Its decisive role in the overthrow of dictatorship in the 1974 **Revolução dos Cravos** (revolution of carnations) is universally recognised. Home to the great **latifúndios** (large farming estates), the

workers from which support any outlet for their anger at the unfair employment policies, this 'Red' region is the antithesis of its northern mirror-image. As flat as the north is craggy, with its liberal attitudes and weaker religious ties, it is an area whose people are very welcoming, albeit slightly wary of strangers. Highly agricultural – olives, cork, pigs – the colours of the landscape offer every imaginable shade of green, stitched together in a blanket of tranquillity, interspersed with vibrant yellow gorse, exquisite purples and blues and a solid base of earthy russets, chestnut and ochres of rich tilled land; an artist's dream.

Évora, the capital, is sheer poetry – if you can fight through its tourists to see the famous temple of Diana, old university and monastery (now a splendid pousada).

Elvas, on the border with Spain, of great historical importance in bygone battles against the invading Spanish and Arab forces, and it has a fantastic aqueduct.

Borba and Redondo are small one-horse towns, but the wine is worth a taste.

Arraiolos is the home to handmade tapestries and rugs, and exquisite blue and white dwellings.

The Algarve
Down into the Algarve, away from the hassle of tourist boom towns the area offers a variety of trips into the hills of Monchique, a spa town sporadically damaged by forest fires. From Lagos and Cape St Vincent, from whence

sailed the navigators of old, to Silves, Tavira and Vila Real on the Spanish border, a car journey can whisk you away from time-share touts, and English grub signs, to a tranquil, colourful environment, especially so in early Spring, when the orange and almond blossom make this part of Portugal an exquisite place to visit.

Regional Directory

The following useful addresses and contact details for three main areas of Portugal (Oporto district, Lisbon, Algarve) provide information pertinent to the ex-pat community. You may find networking easier if you start with fellow compatriots, and support may be facilitated for a number of everyday situations. Further, general and national, contact details are listed in the next section, including UK addresses of various organisations.

A free support line for tourists is available by ringing (0800) 296 296. Information is available on accommodation, travel, events and much more.

OPORTO DISTRICT

I highly recommend getting hold of the publication *Welcome to Porto* published by the Oporto Mothers' Group. See below. The telephone area code for Porto is 22.

Consulates and Foreigners' Dept.

Great Britain: Avenida da Boavista 3072, Porto. Tel: 6184789.

Also at: Quinta de Santa Maria, Estrada de Tavereve, 3030, Figueira da Foz.

France: Rua de Eugénio de Castro, 280 1-s/136 Porto. Tel: 6094584.

Germany: Avenida da Boavista 5004, Porto. Tel: 6102326.

Serviço de Estrangeiros e Fronteiras, Rua D João IV, 536, 4000 Porto. Tel: 5104308/5104384.
Branch office also at: Sub Delegação de Espinho, Rua 19,342-3, Espinho. Tel: 7341165.

Tourist Information

Posto de Turismo, Praça D.João, Porto. Tel: 2057514.
Airport Office. Tel: 9412534.

Business networks

Oporto Chamber of Commerce, Edifício da Bolsa, Rua Ferreira Borges, 4000 Porto. Tel: 200 4497.
Assoc. Luso-Britânico do Porto, Rua do Breiner 155-165, 4000 Porto.

Places of worship

St James Anglican Church (Church of England), Largo da Maternidade Júlio Dinis, 4050, Porto. Contact: Rev. Howell Sasser, Tel: 6091006.
Methodist Church, Igreja Evangélica Portuguesa, Rua Padre José Pacheco do Monte, 308, Porto. Contact: Rev. Peter Clark, Tel: 822780.
Sinagoga Kadooric (Porto Synagogue), 340 Guerra Junqueiro. Tel: 609 2789.

Culture

British Council – library, videos, internet access – Rua do Breiner 155, 4050 Porto. Tel: 2073060. Fax: 2073068.
Instituto Alemão Goetheinstitut (German Goethe Institute), Av.da Boavista 919, 4100 Porto. Tel: 6008120.
Livraria Britânica, (good bookshop) José Falcão 184, Porto. Tel: 3322232.

Sports and hobbies

Oporto Cricket and Lawn Tennis Club (different types of membership available. Several sports facilities and functions and also home to groups such as bridge, aerobics, Oporto Ladies Guild). Details of all activities from: The Club Secretary, OC&LTC, Rua Campo Alegre, 4150, Porto. Tel: 6067323.

The Friends of America Club (various activities, plus regular newsletter). Contact: Ralph Schwartz, Tel: 830 3452.

The Douro Golf Society: contact via the OC&LTC.

Support groups

Porto Mothers' Group meets regularly on Wednesday mornings at St James' Anglican Church Hall, Porto, and has an international membership. Contact: Zoe Harrap, Rua Luís de Camões 263, Miramar, 4405-088 Arcozelo VNG. Tel/fax: 753 1843.

The Bon Marché charity shop (sells clothing and other items, volunteers always welcome), Av.da Boavista 3072, 4100 Porto. Contact: Winnie Soares, Tel: 6173827.

Community Care Group (care of young and elderly. Volunteers or people in need of support). Tel: Olivia Cobb 7640210 or Annie Baker 7121345.

Places of interest

Chiqui Park, Rua Brito Capelo 1119, Matosinhos. Tel: 9377647. Play park for children aged 2 to 10.

Rosa Mota Stadium, situated in the Alameda das Tílias. Huge park and sports arena.

Fundação de Serralves, Rua de Serralves 977, Porto. Tel: 6180057. Beautiful gardens with fountains and animals. Home to Museum of Modern Art, also has a tea room.

Vista Douro river cruises, Rua de Sousa Arosa 352, Matosinhos. Tel: 9387949/ Fax: 9387950.

Education

Karen's Kindergarten, Av. Marechal Gomes da Costa 822. Ages 2–5. Contact Karen Candeias. Tel: 617 6178.

The Garden Nursery, Quinta de Lavadores, Rua Dr. Eduardo Torres, Matosinhos. From age 2½. Contact Lila Wall. Tel: 9383217.

Floresta Mágica, Estrada Cima, 209, Arcozelo. Age 3–5. Contact Isabelle/Isaura. Tel: 7620592.

Language Schools

Inlingua – Escola de Línguas, Edifício do Jornal de Notícias, Rua Gonçalo Cristovão, 217 12 floor, Porto. Tel: 2059313. Fax: 316586.
Email: inlingua@mail.telepac.pt and see www.inlingua.com

Lancaster College, Pct.25 de Abril, 35-1 esq., Vila Nova de Gaia. Tel: 3756495. Fax: 3757201.

Cial centro de Línguas, Rua Passos Manuel, 222-5, Porto. Tel: 3320269. Fax: 2083907.

LISBON

I recommend getting hold of the publication *Feeling at Home in Portugal*, published by the International Women in Portugal Organisation, Apartado 1060, 2750 Cascais, Lisbon. The telephone area code for Lisbon is 21.

Consulates and Foreigners' Dept.

British Embassy, Rua São Domingos à Lapa, 35-37, 1200

Lisboa.

Embassy Consular Section, Rua de São Bernardo 33, 1200 Lisboa. Tel: 392 4160.

British Consulate, Rua da Estrela 4, 1200 Lisboa.

Foreigners' Dept. Rua Cons. José Silvestre Ribeiro 4, 1600 Lisboa. Tel: 7141027.

Tourist information

Main turismo: Palácio Foz, Praça dos Restauradores, Lisboa. Tel: 342 5231/342 34636.

Cascais: Rua Visconde da Luz. Tel: 486 8204.

Estoril: Arcadas do Parque. Tel: 466 3813.

Óbidos: Rua Direita. Tel: 959231.

Peniche: Rua Alexandre Herculano. Tel: 789571.

Sintra: Praça da República 23. Tel: 923 1157.

Évora: Praça do Giraldo. Tel: 22671.

Business networks

Royal British Club (social and business club), Apartado 126, 2765 Estoril. Tel: 468 1712. Fax: 468 1674.

Portuguese-UK Chamber of Commerce, Rua da Estrela 8, 1200 Lisboa.

Lisbon Chamber of Commerce, Rua de Santo Antão 88, Lisboa.

Places of worship

St George's Church, Rua de São Jorge, 6, Lisboa. Tel: 396 3010.

St Andrew's Church of Scotland, Rua Arriaga, 13, Lisboa. Tel: 395 7677.

Setúbal Anglican Church, Rua Cap.Ten. Carvalho Araújo, 15, Setúbal. Tel: 235 0345.

Irish Dominican Community, St Mary's parish centre,

Rua do Murtal, 368, São Pedro do Estoril. Tel: 467 3771.

St Sebastian's Chapel, Parque Castro Guimarães, Rua Boca do Inferno, Cascais.

German Catholic Church, Rua do Patrocínio, 8, Lisboa. Tel: 396 4114.

Lisbon Synagogue, Rua Alexandre Herculano 59, Lisboa. Tel: 385 8604.

Salvation Army, various corps around Lisbon. For details contact Colares Corp, Avenida Bombeiros Voluntários, Colares. Tel: 929 1077.

Riverside International Church, meets at St Julian's School. Contact Pastor Dwight Seletzky. Tel: 443 1202.

Ocean Christian Community, Hotel Atlântico, Monte Estoril. Tel: 442 1897.

Culture

Livraria Britânica (good bookshop), Rua São Marcal, 168-A, 1200 Lisboa. Tel: 342 8472.

Bookstop, English bookshop with book ordering service. Escritório – Estoril, Rua de Lisboa 1C, 2765 Estoril. Tel: 466 0621. Fax: 468 7105.

The British Council Library, Rua Luís Fernandes 3, Lisboa. Tel: 347 6141.

Anglo-American Library, Hotel Atlântico, Monte Estoril, Lisboa.

The British Council, Rua de São Marcal 174, 1294 Lisboa. Tel: 347 6141. Fax: 347 6152.

Sports and hobbies

Continuing education sessions in subjects such as: aerobics, ballet, cello. Contact: Fernanda Knapp, Continuing Education Officer, St Julian's School, Quinta Nova, 2775 Carcavelos Codex. Tel: 456 6817.

The International Music Centre, orchestra for young musicians. Contact: Stephanie Duarte, Outeiro de Polima Arneiro, 2775 São Domingos de Rana. Tel: 444 0434.

Garden Centre Linhó, Quinta da Eira, Centro de Jardinagem Lda. Tel: 923 5263.

Lisbon Casuals Sports Club – details from St Julian's School, Carcavelos. Tel: 456 3618.

Grupo Dramático e Desportivo de Cascais (Drama and Sports Group), Pavilhão dos Desportes, Cascais. Tel: 486 4012.

Quinta da Marinha Village Resort – golf, tennis and much more. Quinta da Marinha, Casa 36, 2750 Cascais. Tel: 486 9881/Fax: 486 9032.

Friends of Montserrate – Assoc. Amigos de Montserrate, R.Augusto dos Santos, 2-4, 1000 Lisboa. Tel: 726 4360.

Support groups

International Women in Portugal: see address at start of section.

American Women of Lisbon (AWOL). Meets at Grand Hotel, Av.Saboia, Monte Estoril. Tel: 486 7297.

International Toddlers Group, Centro Paroquial do Estoril, Av.D. Afonso Henriques 1760, 2765 Estoril. Meets Thursdays 10–12.

Amigos de Lisboa (Friends of Lisbon – Portuguese-speaking group), Palácio de Mitra, Rua do Açúcar, 1900 Lisboa. Tel: 868 5711.

Riding for the disabled. Tel: 483 2147/ 483 7486.

Welcome Relocation Tel/Fax: 924 0448.

Cheshire Home, Lar da Boa Vontade, Av. do Loureiro 251A, Carcavelos. Tel: 457 9082 or 395 1634.

Pregnancy support group, contact Anne Cockerham on 456-3125.

Places of interest

The monastery at Alcobaça, Mosteiro de Santa Maria de Alcobaça, Praça 25 de Abril, Alcobaça. Tel: 43469.

Boca do Inferno (the mouth of hell), Av. Rei Humberto de Itália, Cascais.

The National Palace of Queluz, Largo do Palácio, 2745 Queluz. Tel: 435 0039.

Pena Palace, Estrada da Pena, Sintra. Tel: 923 0227.

Aldeia de José Franco (miniature village, with playground). Sobreiro, 2640 Mafra. Tel: 52420.

Roman ruins at Conímbriga, just south of Condeixa-a-Nova (north from Lisbon). Tel: 941177.

Onda Parque (Waterpark), Costa da Caparica – south over bridge from Lisbon. Suitable for older children. Tel: 295-1120.

Portugal dos Pequeninos: scale models of Portugal's monuments. Great day out. Santa Clara, Coimbra. Tel: 441225.

Pavilion of the Oceans – Oceanarium on the Expo 98 site. Biggest in Europe.

Education

Miss Rita Croft da Moura, Rua Arriaga 13, 1200 Lisboa. Tel: 397 8603. Age 3–6.

Queen Elizabeth School, R.Filipe Magalhães 1, Alvalade, 1700 Lisboa. Tel: 848 6928, Fax: 847 2513. Age 3–11.

St George's School, Av. do Lidador 322, São João do Estoril, 2765 Estoril. Tel: 466 1774. Age 3–13.

Language schools

Linguarama, Av. da Liberdade 49, 5 piso, 1250-227 Lisboa. Tel: 342 6350, Fax: 342 6351.
See: www.linguarama.pt

Cambridge School, Av.da Liberdade 173, 1250 Lisboa. Tel: 312 4600, Fax: 353 4729.
Email: cambridge@mail.telepac.pt
See www.cambridge.pt

Speakwell – Escola de Línguas, Praça Mário de Azevedo Gomes, Lote 12-1, 2775-240 Parede. Tel: 456 1775. Fax: 456 1771. Email: speakwell@mail.telepac.pt

THE ALGARVE

The Algarve Resident journal is published each Friday and is a good source of information on local activities. You can buy it widely across the Algarve.

Consulates and Foreigners' Dept.

British Consulate, Largo Francisco A.Mauricio 7-1, 8500 Portimão. Tel: 282-417800/ 417804.

Foreigners' Dept, Rua Dr José de Matos 14, 8000 Faro. Tel: 289-805822.

Tourist information

Albufeira: R.5 de Outubro, 8200 Albufeira. Tel: 289-512144.

Armação de Pêra: Av. Marginal, 8365 Arm. De Pêra. Tel: 282-312145.

Carvoeiro: Largo Praia do Carvoeiro, 8400 Carvoeiro, LGA. Tel: 282-357728.

Faro: Rua da Misericórdia 8-12, 8000 Faro. Tel: 289-803604.

Lagos: Largo Marquês de Pombal, 8600 Lagos. Tel: 282-763031.

Loulé: Edifício do Castelo, 8100 Loulé. Tel: 289-463900.

Monte Gordo: Av.Marginal, 8900 Monte Gordo. Tel: 281-44495.

Portimão: Largo 1 de Dezembro, 8500 Portimão. Tel: 282-23695.

Praia da Rocha: Av.Tomás Cabreira, 8500 Praia da Rocha. Tel: 282-22290.

Silves: Rua 25 de Abril, 8300 Silves. Tel: 282-442255.

Business networks

Network: The Association of Working and Business Women. Contact: Margaret Ellis Tel: 282-697190.

Blueprint Media Enterprises Ltd (organise useful seminars). Tel: 282-342506. Fax: 282-342939.

Lions Clube de Loulé. Contact: Mi on 289-314286, or Gerard on 289-845581.

Assoc. of Foreign Property Owners in Portugal (AFPOP), Apartado 728, 8501-917 Portimão. Tel: 282-458509. Fax: 282-458277. Email: afpop@mail.telepac.pt

Portuguese-UK Chamber of Commerce in the Algarve: contact London office on (020) 7494 1844.

Places of worship

RC Mass, Block H 1st floor, Torralta, Alvor. Saturdays at 6pm.

Salvation Army, São Bras, Rua 25 de Abril, Lote 19. Tel: 289-841126.

St Vincent's Anglican Chaplaincy, various districts.

Details from Churchwarden. Tel: 282-338553 (Central district).

International Christian Fellowship Baptist Church, Av. 25 de Abril, 17 r/c-D, Portimão. Tel: 282-495243.

Lagoa Christian Fellowship, meets in Carvoeiro. Tel: 282-357190.

The International Evangelical Church of the Algarve, meets in Vale Judeu. Tel: 289-328635.

Manna Church, Urb. Caldeira do Moinho. Lote 1A Portimão. Tel: 282-414066.

Seventh Day Adventist Church, various locations. Tel: 282-492051.

Jewish Religious Notices, Tel: 282-416710.

Dutch Protestant church, Restaurant Carrusel, Praia d'Ouro, Albufeira, Sundays at 10.30.

Culture

Griffin Bookshop (excellent shop and services, including rapid order system and local regular bookfair). Rua 5 de Outubro, 206A, 8135 Almancil. Tel: 289-393904. Fax: 289-399632.
Email: griffin@mail.telepac.pt

Sports and hobbies

The Algarveans Experimental Theatre. Contact: Jean Broad. Tel: 282-461398. Fax: 282-461399.

Parque da Floresta Golf and leisure resort. Contact: Grant Woodgate. Tel: 282-697321.
Internet: www.vigiasa.com

Car boot sales: various locations. Tel: 289-399107.

Line dancing, Portimão Gymnasium. Tel: 282-496070.

Chess Club, Nucleo xadrez. Tel: 282-342982.

Art lessons, Studio Camilo Artes. Tel: 282-760129.
Piano/keyboard lessons. Contact: Josephine Sands. Tel: 289-366720.
Almancil Hash Harriers (running). Tel: 289-328209.

Support groups

Alcoholics Anonymous: Albufeira: contact Jimmy 91-9109986/Jan 289-489563. Portimão: contact Barry 282-788260. Pêra: contact Jerry or Leta Rae on 289-413418/91-9718613.

Moms and Tots group, Kidsplay, Rua do Comércio 48, Almancil. Tel: 93-3313832.

Mums and Toddlers group, Igreja Baptista church hall, Av 25 de Abril, Portimão. Tel: 282-485243.

Animal Rescue Centre, APPA, Alcalar, Portimão. Tel: 282-471347.

Mind, Body and Soul (aromatherapy, reflexology and massage). Sede No Lote 53A, Vale Verde, Quinta do Lago, 8135 Almancil. Tel: 289-392218.

Counselling – Tel: 282-471479

Places of interest

Portitours (activity days), Rua Teófilo Braga, Edifício Pluma, Loja 2P, 8500 Portimão. Tel: 282-417978.

The Mines of Alcoutim, Assoc. Alcance, Assoc. para o Desenvolvimento do Concelho de Alcoutim, Rua 1 de Maio, Alcoutim. Tel: 281-46428.

Useful Contacts

These contacts are in addition to any already mentioned in the main part of the book. The order follows the chapter structure of the book for easier reference. The list is not exhaustive and further information can always be sought from the relevant departments and bodies.

> **Portugal – Telephone numbers in Portugal changed on 1 November 1999. For area codes in the Algarve the initial '0' has been replaced by a '2', hence the old code for Faro (089) became 289-, etc. The Lisbon code changed from 01- to 21-, and Oporto from 02- to 22-. All other areas experienced a similar change. All attempts have been made to supply the correct codes, but should you dial a former area code number, Portugal Telecom will announce the new code to you.**

OFFICIALDOM

Portuguese Embassy, 11 Belgrave Square, London SW1Z 8PP. Tel: (020) 7235 5331.

Portuguese Consulate General, Silver City House, 62 Brompton Rd, London SW3 1BJ. Tel: (020) 7.581 8722.

Also at:

The Portuguese Consulate, Alexandra Court, 93 Princess Street, Manchester M1 4HT. Tel: (0161) 834 1821.

The Portuguese Consulate, 25 Bernard Street, Edinburgh EH6 6SH. Tel: (0131) 555 2080.

Honorary Consul, Hurst House, 15-19 Corporation Street, Belfast BT1 3HA. Tel: (01232) 242242.

Honorary Consul, 4 Knoll Court, Sneyd Park, Bristol BS9 1QX. Tel: (01272) 685042.

The Portuguese Consulate, 2nd Floor, 14 Conway Street, St.Helier, Jersey, CI. Tel: (015348) 77188.

Ministry of Agriculture, Fisheries and Food, Nobel House, 17 Smith Square, London SW1P 3HX. Tel: (020) 7238 3000.

Ministry of Agriculture, Animal Health Division IC (taking pets abroad), Hook Rise South, Tolworth, Surbiton, Surrey KT6 7NF. Tel: (020) 8330 4441.

European Commission Office, 8 Storey Gate, London SW1P 3AT. Tel: (020) 7973 1992. Fax: (020) 7973 1900.

Blair Consular services (visas), 9 City Business Centre, Lower Rd, London SE16 2XB. Tel: (020) 7252 1451.

Lisbon Customs and Excise, Direcção Geral das Alfândegas, R.Terreiro Trigo, 1100 Lisboa. Tel: 21-888 3576.

Ministry of Agriculture, Praça do Comércio, 1100 Lisboa. Tel: 21-342 7597.

Bureaucratic Help Service, Rua das Lapas, CC Charneca, Loja 13, Charneca, 2750 Cascais. Tel: 21-485 8230.

TRAVEL

ICEP The Portuguese Trade and Tourism Office, 22-25a Sackville Street, London W1X 1PE. Tel: (020) 7494

5720. www.portugalinsite.pt

Email: tourism@portugaloffice.org.uk

TAP Air Portugal, Gillingham House, 38/44 Gillingham Street, London SW1P 4NP. Tel: 0845-601-0932. www.TAP-AirPortugal.pt

Caravela (TAP subsidiary), as above. Tel: (020) 7630 9223.

Brittany Ferries, Millbay Docks, Plymouth, Devon PL1 3EW. Tel: (0990) 360360.

P&O European Ferries, The Continental Ferry Port, Mile End, Portsmouth PO2 8QW. Tel: (0990) 980980.

British Rail Continental Section, Victoria Station, London SW1. Tel: (020) 7834 2345.

Voyages Jules Verne, 21 Dorset Square, London NW1 6QG. Tel: (020) 7616 1000. Fax: (020) 7723 8629. www.vjv.co.uk

EHS Travel (beautiful hotel-fort near Cascais). Tel: 01993-700600. www.ehstravel.co.uk

Simply Travel (Portugal & Madeira). Tel: (020) 8541 2222. www.simplytravel.com

Holiday homes in Northern Portugal, Adrian and Lucina Phillips. Tel: (01985) 213409.

Email: aris.phillips@btinternet.com

Alternative Travel Group, 69-71 Banbury Road, Oxford OX2 6PE. Tel: (01865) 315680. Fax: (01865) 310299 (walking holidays).

Portugália Airlines, PGA, Olympic House, Manchester Airport, Manchester M90 1QX. Tel: (0990) 502048.

Abreu Travel Agency Ltd, 109 Westbourne Grove, London W2 4UW. Tel: (020) 7229 9905. Fax: (020) 7229 0274. Email: abreu.mail@btinternet.com

Latitude 40, 13 Beauchamp Place, Knightsbridge, London SW3 1NQ. Tel: (020) 7581 3104. Fax: (020)

7589 5409.

Portugalia Holidays, 94 Fortis Green Road, London N2 9EY. Tel: (020) 8444 1857.

Condor Travel (UK) Ltd, 234 Earls Court Road, London SW5 9AA. Tel: (020) 7373 0495. Fax: (020) 7835 1052. Email: Gio@Condor-Travel.co.uk

Faro Airport. Tel: 289-818281.

Lisbon Airport. Tel: 21-841 3700.

Stagecoach Portugal, Lisbon. Tel: 21-483 2055.

Assoc. of Travel Agents and Tourism, (APAVT), Rua Duque de Palmela 2-1 Dto, 1200 Lisboa. Tel: 21-352 9468. Fax: 21-314 5080.

Instituto de Promoção Turística, Rua Alexandre Herculano 51-2, 1200 Lisboa. Tel: 21-681174.

Direcção Geral do Turismo, Av. António Augusto de Aguiar 86, 1069-021 Lisboa. Tel: 21-357 5086. Fax: 21-315 0308. www.dgturismo.pt

CP- Caminhos de Ferro Portugueses (National Railways), for info on services and timetables, Av.da República 66, 1000 Lisboa. Tel: 21-793 1633. www.cp.pt

REMOVALS

The British Assoc. of Removers, 3 Churchill Court, 58 Station Road, North Harrow, Middlesex HA2 7SA. Tel: (020) 8861 3331. Fax: (020) 8861 3332. Email: movers@bar.co.uk

Robert Darvall Ltd, 4 Acre Road, Reading, Berkshire RG1 0SX. Tel: (01734) 864422.

Almar Transportes, 131 Westbourne Park Rd, London W2. Tel: (020) 7243 1905.

Trans-Portugal European, 59 St Thomas Street, London SE1. Tel: (020) 7403 1440.

Reis International Transport, Double 4, 54 Neasden Lane, London NW10. Tel: (020) 7372 0817.

Northovers Removals and Storage, Passfield Mill Business Park, Passfield, near Liphook, Hants. GU30 7RR. Tel: (01428) 751554. Fax: (01428) 751564.

Fleet Shipping International Ltd, Tel: (020) 7232 0777. Fax: (020) 7232 2600. Email: sales@fleet.demon.co.uk and see www.fleet-shipping.co.uk

Overs International, Unit 8, Government Road Industrial Park, Government Rd, Aldershot GU11 2DA. Tel: (01252) 343646. Fax: (01252) 345861.

Gauntlett International Removals Ltd, Gauntlett House, Catteshall Rd, Godalming, Surrey GU7 1NH. Tel: (01483) 417766.

The Old House (Removals and Warehousing) Ltd, London. Tel: (020) 8947 1817. Also at: 15-17 High Street, Seaford, East Sussex BN25 1PD. Tel: (01323) 892934.

Ferry Freighting (Manchester) Ltd, Ferry House, 24-26 Brook St, Chedderton, Oldham OL9 6NN. Tel: (0161) 626 8686.

Charles M Willie & Co (Shipping) Ltd, Celtic House, Brittania Rd, Cardiff CF1 5LS. Tel: (01222) 471000.

Transports Reis/Portugal Travel, 84 York St, London W1. Tel: (020) 7723 7774.

Copsey Removals, 178 Crow Lane, Romford, Essex RM7 0ES. Tel: (020) 8592 1003. Fax: (01708) 727305.

Avalon Overseas, Drury Way, Brent Park, London NW10 0JN. Tel: (020) 8451 6336. Fax: (020) 8451 6419. Email: avalon@transeuro.com

Bishops Move, Overseas House, Stewarts Rd, London SW8 4UG. Tel: (020) 7498 0300. Fax: (020) 7498 0749. Email: www.bishopsmove.co.uk

Britannia, 1 Pegasus Road, Croydon, Surrey, CR0 4RN.
(020) 8256 1700. Fax: (020) 8336 0961.
Email: www.britannia_movers.co.uk
Gauntlett International Transportes Lda, Estrada Nacio-
nal 125, 8400 Lagos, Algarve.
Corporate Relocations & Personal Relocations, Apt.432,
8135 Almancil, Algarve.
AJ Gonçalves de Morães Lda, PO Box 2772, Rua de São
Paulo 26, 1200 Lisboa.

ACCOMMODATION
Youth Hostels Association, 14 Southampton St, London
WC2.
RCI Europe Ltd (Timeshare), Clarendon House, Station
Rd, Kettering, Northants NN15 7QT. Tel: (01536)
310101.
ENATUR (Pousadas), Av.Santa Joana Princesa 10A,
1700 Lisboa. Tel: 21-844 2001. www.pousadas.pt
Manor Houses of North Portugal, PRIVETUR, Largo
das Pereiras, 4990 Ponte de Lima. Tel: 741493.
Assoc. Portuguesa de Pousadas de Juventude (Youth Hos-
tels), MOVIJOVEM, Av.Duque D'Ávila 137, 1050
Lisboa. Tel: 21-3559081. Fax: 21-3528621.
Direcção Geral do Turismo, Av.António Augusto de
Aguiar 86, 1099 Lisboa Codex.

PROPERTY AGENTS
Cambridge Trading International Ltd, 83-85 Dunstable
Street, Ampthill, Bedford MK45 2NQ. Tel: (01525)
405900.
Casinhas Portugal Ltd, Goleigh Farm, Selborne,
Hampshire GU34 3SE. Tel: (01420) 511538.

Property Search Portugal, The Gables, Bell Lane, Cassington, Witney, Oxon. OX8 1DS. Tel: (01865) 883154. Fax: (01865) 883301.

Aimcliff Properties, 5-9 Station Rd, Hornchurch, Essex RM12 6JL. Tel: (020) 7435 1480. Fax: (020) 7435 1478.

Cerro Novo Lda, The Manor House, Edington, Westbury, Wiltshire BA13 4QW. Tel: (01380) 831411. Fax: (01380) 831455.

Jones Lang Wootton, 22 Hanover Square, London W1A 2BN. Tel: (020) 7493 6040. Fax: (020) 7493 9539.

Mike Hough Associates (Agricultural), The Laurels, Mill Road, Bintree, Dereham, Norfolk NR20 5NL. Tel: (01362) 683790. Fax: (01362) 684175.

Prime Property International, 7 High St, Maidenhead, Berkshire SL6 1JN. Tel: (01628) 778841. Fax: (01628) 35052.

Pugh Homes, 42 Walcott Av, Christchurch, Dorset BH23 2NG. Tel/Fax: (01202) 487396.

Roy Grant & Co, 1 Albert St, Aberdeen AB1 1XX. Tel: (01224) 645066. Fax: (01224) 642525.

IDANA – Algarve Imobiliária Lda, Rua João de Deus 43, 8250 São Brás de Alportel, Algarve. Tel: 289-842369.

S&E – Saviotti & Esaguy, Rua Marquês da Fronteira 76-7, 1070 Lisboa. Tel: 387-0441.

IN's, Av.Eng.Duarte Pacheco, Torre 2-5, Sala 9, Amoreiras, 1070 Lisboa. Tel: 383-2777.

Globinveste, Av.Barbosa Bocage 106-1, 1050 Lisboa. Tel: 795-0780.

Fernandes & Costa Lda (represented by Bailey & Ambler, Grantham), Av.Almirante Reis 104-2, 1100 Lisboa.

Tel: 812-3231.

José Santos Lda, Rua dos Corrieiros 101-1, 1100 Lisboa. Tel: 346-0707.

Predial Zela Lda, Rua António Maria Cardoso 15-1, 1200 Lisboa. Tel: 347-5448.

Cicerone (represented by Palmer & Parker, London), Av.-dos Bombeiros Voluntários, 4, 2765 Estoril. Tel: 468-0389.

Movi, Agência Imobiliária Lda (represented by Palmer & Parker), Av.Marginal 9348, 1 Esq, 2750 Cascais. Tel: 483-1032.

Agência Vitoria, Rua Regimento Dezanove, 81 r/c, 2750 Cascais. Tel: 483-3230.

LEGAL

Figuereido & Co, Berkeley House, 3rd floor, 73 Upper Richmond Rd, London SW15 2SZ. Tel: (020) 8877 3844. Fax: (020) 8877 0556.

Lourdes Prazes, 70 Ashburnham Rd, London NW1O. Tel: (020) 8960 0948. Fax: (020) 8969 8920.

Lita Gale Solicitors, 43-45 Gower St, London WC1E 6HH. Tel: (020) 7580 2066. Fax: (020) 7580 2067.

Harris da Silva Advogados, 355 City Rd, London EC1V 1RL. Tel: (020) 7713 0700.

Neville de Rougemont e Associados, City Cloisters, Suite C4, 188-196 Old St, London EC1V 8BP. Tel: (020) 7490 4656 (also in Lagos and Lisbon).

Barros, Sobral, Xavier and G Gomes – UK, New Loom House, 101 Back Church Lane, London E1 1LU. Tel: (020) 7488 0933.

Noronha Advogados, Suite 1, 52 Ennismore Gardens, London SW7 1AH. Tel: (020) 7581 5040.

José Bulha International Law Offices, Rua Bartolomeu Dias, Lote 7D – 3, Cerro Alagoa, 8200 Albufeira. Tel: 289-586104. Fax: 289-515786.

William Oddy Sampson & Co, Praça da República 12- 3 esq, 8800 Tavira, Algarve (also in Lagoa and Almancil).

Maria Teresa Silva & Associados, Av.Conde Valbom 82-6 Dto, 1000 Lisboa.

Mr R P Duarte, Rua João Grave 125, 1 FTR. 16, 4100 Porto.

FINANCIAL

Allan Wright (Canada Life Assurance Co), Albany House, Dollis Mews, Dollis Park, Finchley, London N3 1HH. Tel: (020) 8346 2651.

Ronald M Collins & Co, Chartered Accountants, Downs Court Business Centre, 29 The Downs, Altrincham, Cheshire WA14 2QD. Tel: (0161) 941 2868.

Blackstone Franks, Barbican House, 26-34 Old Street, London EC1V 9HL. Tel: (020) 7250 3300.

Brown Shipley Lomond Ltd, 84 Coombe Rd, New Malden, Surrey KT3 4QS. Tel: (020) 8949 8811.

Expat Tax Consultants, Churchfield House, North Drive, Hebburn, Tyne & Wear NE31 1ES. Tel: (0191) 483 7805.

Hall-Godwins Overseas, Briarcliff House, Kingsmead, Farnborough, Hants GU14 7TE. Tel: (01252) 521701.

Seatax Ltd (tax advisers), 100 East Iaith Gate, Doncaster DN1 1JA. Tel: (01302) 364673.

Bone & Co Insurance Brokers, 69A Castle St, Farnham, Surrey GU9 7LP. Tel: 01252-724140.

Dave Tester Expatriate Insurance Services, 18A Hove

Park Villas, Hove BN3 6HG. Tel: (01273) 703469. Fax: (01273) 777723. Email: dave.tester@compuserve.com

Expatriate Advisory Services, 14 Gordon Rd, West Bridgeford, Nottingham NG2 5LN. Tel: (01602) 816572.

Expats International, 29 Lacon Rd, London SE22 9HE. Tel: (020) 8229 2484.

Wilfred T. Fry Ltd, Crescent House, Crescent Rd, Worthing BN11 1RN. Tel: (01903) 231545. Fax: (01903) 200868.

Suzan Stolk Insurance, Apt.369, 2751-905 Cascais. Tel: 21-487 0819.

The Royal Bank of Scotland (Gibraltar) Ltd, 1 Corral Road, Gibraltar. Tel: Gibraltar 73200. Fax: 70152.

Companhia de Seguros Tranquilidade, Av. da Liberdade 242, 1250 Lisboa. Tel: 356-1181.

Companhia Europeia de Seguros Lda, Av. Fontes Pereira de Melo, 6-11, 1050 Lisboa. Tel: 353-3376.

Companhia de Seguros Sun Alliance Portugal, Av.5 de Outubro 146-7, 1050 Lisboa. Tel: 797-8819.

American Life Insurance Company, Av. da Liberdade 36-4, 1250 Lisboa. Tel: 347-5031.

Royal Insurance Plc, Rua Castilho 50-1, 1250 Lisboa. Tel: 386-3634.

Scottish Union, Rua Brancaamp, 11, 1250 Lisboa. Tel: 350-3700.

BANKS

Barclays Bank Plc, International Banking Group, 168 Fenchurch Street, London EC3P 3HP. Tel: (020) 7283 8989.

Banco Totta & Açores SA, 68 Cannon Street, London EC4N 6AQ. Tel: (020) 7236 1515. Fax: (020) 7329 3582.

Banco Espirito Santo e Comercial de Lisboa, 33 Queen Street, London EC4R 1ES. Tel: (020) 7332 4300. Fax: (020) 7332 4340.

Banco Nacional Ultramarino (BNU), 7th floor, Walbrook House, 23 Walbrook, London EC4N 8BT. Tel: (020) 7280 0200. Fax: (020) 7280 0201.

Banco Pinto & Sotto Mayor, 5th floor, 10 Philpot Lane, London EC3M 8AA. Tel: (020) 7626 5021.

Banco Português do Atlântico, 17 Cheapside, London EC3. Tel: (020) 7626 1711.

Banco de Portugal, Rua do Comércio 148, 1100 Lisboa. Tel: 21-346 2931.

EMPLOYMENT SERVICES

Monarch Catering Agency (has recruitment branches in Portugal), 133 Allington St, Victoria, London SW1E 5EB. Tel: (020) 7828 9955. Fax: (020) 7931 0030. Email: gdp95@dial.pipex.com

FRES – Federation of Recruitment and Employment Services Ltd, 36-38 Mortimer St, London W1N 7RB.

CEPEC Ltd, 67 Jermyn St, London SW1Y 6NY. Tel: (020) 7930 0322.

Publicitas Ltd, 525 Fulham Rd, London SW6. Tel: (020) 7385 7723.

Eagle Recruitment, 57 Brompton Rd, London SW3 1DP. Tel: (020) 7823 9233.

International Secretaries, 174 New Bond St, London W1Y 9PB.

EGOR – Recursos Humanos, Rua Castilho 74-4 esq,

1250 Lisboa.

Valor Humano, Rua da Boavista 83-3, 1200 Lisboa. Tel: 21-395 1587.

SELGEC – Rua Alexandre Herculano 30 r/c esq, 1200 Lisboa. Tel: 21-540534

Glasford, Av.Duque D'Ávila 185-8, 1050-082 Lisboa. Tel: 21-315 5955. Fax: 21-315 5818. Email: glasford@mail.telepac.pt

Creyf Portugal, Travessa do Carmo, 4 r/c, 1200 Lisboa. Tel: 347-2061.

SEQUIL, Rua de Buenos Aires, 5 c/v-B, 1200 Lisboa. Tel: 395-7242.

MANPOWER, Praça José Fontana, 9/c, 1050 Lisboa. Tel: 313-4000.

Hospedeiras de Portugal, Rua Borges Carneiro, 42-1 esq, 1200 Lisboa. Tel: 395-1372.

Eurocede, Rua das Lusíadas, 58A, 1300 Lisboa. Tel: 363-0968.

Tax/work depts

Dept. for Education and Employment (DfEE), Sanctuary Buildings, Great Smith Street, London SW1P 3BT. Tel: (020) 7925 5555. Email: info@dfee.gov.uk

Employment Services, Overseas Placing Unit, (OPS5), Moorfoot, Sheffield, S1 4PQ.

Inland Revenue, Inspector of Foreign Dividends, Lynwood Rd, Thames Ditton, Surrey.

DGCI Direcção Geral de Contribuições e Impostos, Rua da Alfândega 5, 1100 Lisboa. Tel: 21-887 9961.

Ministério do Emprêgo e Segurança Social, Praça de Londres 2, 1000 Lisboa. Tel: 21-847 0430.

BUSINESS/TRADE ASSOCIATIONS

Portuguese-UK Chamber of Commerce, 4th floor, 22/25a Sackville Street, London W1X 1DE. Tel: (020) 7494-1844. Fax: (020) 7494-1822.

DTI Portuguese Desk, 8th floor, Kingsgate House, 66-74 Victoria St, London SW1E 6SW.

Portuguese Government Trade Office, New Bond Street House, 1 New Bond St, London W1Y 0DB. Tel: (020) 7493 0212.

Instituto do Investimento Estrangeiro (Foreign Investment Institute), Av.da Liberdade, 258-4, 1200 Lisboa.

Turismo de Lisboa, Visitors and Convention Bureau, Aprt.3326, 1301-904 Lisboa. Tel: 21-361 0350. Fax: 21-361 0359. Email: atl@atl-turismolisboa.pt and see www.atl-turismolisboa.pt

Porto Convention Bureau, Av.Diogo Leite 242, 4400 Vila Nova de Gaia, Porto. Tel: 790071. Fax: 790067. Email: portconv@mail.telepac.pt and see www.porto-convention-bureau.pt

Portuguese Ministry of Foreign Affairs, Consular Section, Largo do Rilvas, 1354 Lisboa Codex.

Assoc. Industrial Portuguesa, Praça das Indústrias, Pavilhão da FIL, 1300 Lisboa.

Eurogabinete (EU info), Av.Casal Ribeiro 59, P-1000 Lisboa.

ACCOUNTANCY FIRMS

Arthur Andersen & Co, 1 Surrey St, London WC2R 2PS. Tel: (020) 7438 3000.

Ernst & Young, Rolls House, 7 Rolls Buildings, Fetter Lane, London EC4A 1NH. Tel: (020) 7831 7130.

KPMG Peat Marwick, 1 Puddle Dock, Blackfriars,

London EC4V 3PD. Tel: (020) 7236 8000.
Price Waterhouse, Av.da Liberdade, 245-7B, 1250 Lisboa.
Tel: 21-311 3300.
Arthur Andersen & Co, Amoreiras, Torre 1-15, 1070 Lisboa. Tel: 21-381 6000.
Ernst & Young, Edifício Republicano, Av.da República 90- 3, 1600 Lisboa.
And at: Rua Gonçalo Sampaio, 271-4 esq, 4150 Porto. Tel: 22-600 2015.
Duncan Macgregor Chartered Accountants, Rua Dr Mário Quina No12, P-2765 Estoril. Tel: 21-466 0045.
Deloitte Ross Tohmatsu, Empreendimento das Amoreiras, Av.Eng. Duarte Pacheco, Torre 1, 12 andar, 1000 Lisboa.

DRIVING
Almar Rent-a-car, 131 Westbourne Park Rd, London W2. Tel: (020) 7243 1905. Email: sales@almar.abcnet.-co.uk
AA, Fanum House, Basingstoke, Hampshire RG21 2EA.
RAC, Landsdowne Rd, Croydon, Surrey CR9 2JA.
Manor Car Storage, PO Box 28, Clavering, Saffron Walden, Essex CB11 4RA. Tel: (01799) 550021.
Automóvel Club de Portugal (ACP), Rua Rosa Araújo 24/6, 1250 Lisboa. Tel: 21-396 3931. www.acp.pt
ACP-Porto, Rua Gonçalo Cristovão 2-6, 4000-263 Porto. Tel: 22-205 6732.
United Textalgarve Lda, (Importing) R. 5 de Outubro 42, Almancil, Algarve. Tel: 289-395747. Fax: 289-395688.
Escola de Condução Portuense (driving school), Rua Alexandre Herculano 311-1, 4000 Porto.

CAMPING

Destination Portugal, Madeira House, 37 Corn St, Witney, Oxon OX8 7BW. Tel: (01993) 773269. Fax: (01993) 771910. www.co.uk/portugal

Premier Holidays, Westbrooke Centre, Milton Rd, Cambridge C4 1YG. Tel: (01223) 516414. Fax: (01223) 516615.

Shearings Holidays, Miry Lane, Wigan, Lancs WN3 4AG. Tel: (01942) 824824. Fax: (01942) 824978.

Information from: www.roteiro-campista.pt and info@roteiro-campista.pt

EDUCATION

European Council of International Schools, 21b Lavant Street, Petersfield, Hants GU2 3EL. Tel: (01730) 268244. Email: ecis@ecis.org

BBC Broadcasting Support Services, 252 Western Ave, London W3 6WJ. Tel: (020) 7992 5522 (info on Portuguese studies in UK).

Higher Educ. – Dept. do Ensino Superior, Ministério da Educação, Av.Duque D'Ávila 137-4, P-1000 Lisboa. Tel: 21-357 5292.

National Institute for Youth, Agência Nacional Instituto Português da Juventude, Av da Liberdade 194, 1250 Lisboa. Tel: 21-315 1961. Fax: 21-315 1959.

Institute of Employment and Professional Training, IEFP, Instituto do Emprego e Formação Profissional, Av. da República 62-7, 1000 Lisboa. Tel: 21-796 9361.

CEARTE – Vocational Training for Handicrafts, Zona Industrial da Pedrulha, Apt.8146, 3020 Coimbra. Tel: 239-492399.

CEFPI Centre for Education and Integrated Vocational

Training, Rua da Vila Nova, 1323, 4100 Porto. Tel: 22-6173378. Fax: 22-6102231.

CENJOR – Protocol Vocational Training for Journalists, R.Júlio de Andrade 5, 1150 Lisboa. Tel: 21-8853786. Fax: 21-8853355.

CESAI Vocational Training for Computer Science, R de Ciriaco Cardoso 186, 4100 Porto. Tel: 22-6101676. Fax: 22-6102051.

Ministério da Educação, Gabinete de Relações Internacionais, Av.5 de Outubro 35-37, 1000 Lisboa.

Cambridge School (EFL), Rua Duque da Terceira 381, Porto.

Cambridge School (EFL), Praça da República 15, Coimbra.

Instituto de Línguas de Faro, Av. 5 de Outubro, Faro.

Language Information

APPA – Assoc. of Teachers of Portuguese to Adults, c/o FXT Fernandes, Goldsmiths College, CCCE, Lewisham Way, London SE14 6NW. Tel: (020) 7919 7200. Email: F.X.Fernandes@gold.ac.uk

Association for Language Learning, 150 Railway Terrace, Rugby CV21 3HN. Tel: (01788) 546443. Fax: (01788) 544149. Email: langlearn@aol.com

Assoc. of Translation Companies, Alexandra House, Alexandra Terrace, Guildford GU1 3DA. Tel: (01483) 456486.

The British Council Information Centre (EFL), 5th floor, Bridgewater House, 58 Whitworth St, Manchester M1 6BB. Tel: (0161) 957 7755. Fax: (0161) 957 7762. Email: general.enquiries@britcoun.org and see www.britcoun.org

CILT Centre for Information on Language Teaching and Research, 20 Bedfordbury, London WC2N 4LB. Tel: (020) 7379 5110. Fax: (020) 7379 5082.
Email: library@cilt.org.uk and see www.cilt.org.uk

International Assoc. of Teachers of EFL (IATEFL), 3 Kingsdown Chambers, Kingsdown Park, Whitstable CT5 2DJ. Tel: (01227) 276528. Fax: (01227) 274415. Email: 100070.1327@compuserve.com
and see www.go-ed.com/jobs/iatefl

OCR (exams in Portuguese), Pat Fellows, Languages, 1 Hills Rd, Cambridge CB1 2EU. Tel: (01223) 553311. Fax: (01223) 460278.

Scottish Assoc. for Language Learning, George Herriott School, Lauriston Place, Edinburgh EH3 9EQ. Tel: (0131) 229 7263.

Grant bodies

Central Bureau, 10 Spring Gardens, London SW1A 2BN. Tel: (020) 7389 4004. Fax: (020) 7389 4426.

HEALTH

Department of Health Leaflets Unit, PO Box 21, Honeypot Lane, Stanmore, Middlesex HA7 1AY. Tel: (0800) 555777.

DSS Benefits Agency, Pensions & Overseas Benefits Directorate, Incapacity Benefits Section, Tyneview Park, Whitely Rd, Newcastle-upon-Tyne NE98 1BA.

Social Security Agency, Incapacity Benefits Branch, Castle Court, Royal Ave, Belfast BT1 1UB.

Royal National Institute for Deaf People, 19-23 Featherstone St, London EC1Y 8SL. Tel: (020) 7296 8000. Fax: (020) 7296 8199. Minicom: (020) 7296 8001.

RNIB, Head Office, 224 Great Portland St, London W1N 6AA. Tel: (020) 7388 1266. Fax: (020) 7388 2034.

Henley Wright Repatriation Services (funerals), 221 Upper Richmond Rd, Putney, London SW15 6SQ. Tel: (020) 8788 5303. Fax: (020) 8788 2525.

Exeter Friendly Society (medical insurance), Beech Hill, Walnut Gardens, Exeter, Devon EX4 4DG. Tel: (01392) 477210.

BUPA International, Russell Mews, Brighton BN7 2NE. Tel: (01273) 208181. Fax: (01273) 866583. Email: www.bupa.com/int

Healthsearch Ltd (medical insurance advice), 9 Newland St, Rugby CV22 7BJ. Tel: (01788) 541855.

PPP, Eynsham House, Tunbridge Wells, Kent TN1 2PL. Tel: (01892) 512345.

Portuguese Pensions Office – Centro Nacional de Pensões, Campo Grande 6, 1771 Lisboa.

International Relations/Social Security Benefits – Departamento de Relações Internacionais e Convenções de Segurança Social, Rua de Junqueira 112, 1302 Lisboa.

Department of Health – Ministério de Saúde, Rua Rodrigo Sampaio, 146 – 3 Dto, 1100 Lisboa.

The British Hospital, Rua Saraiva de Carvalho 49, 1200 Lisboa. Tel: 21-395 5067.

Clínica Médica Internacional de Lisboa, Av.António Augusto de Aguiar 40 r/c esq, 1050 Lisboa. Tel: 21-353 0817.

Clínica Médica Internacional de Cascais, Largo Luis de Camões 67 – 2, Cascais. Tel: 21-484 5317.

Family Medical Centre, Vilar do Golfe 5, Quinta do Lago, Algarve.

Dr.Otfried Gembella, Rua Sotto Major 7 – 2, 8000 Faro.

LuzDoc International Medical Services, Rua 25 de Abril 12, Praia da Luz, Algarve.

Medico Dental Clinic, Hotel Rochas II, Praia da Rocha, Portimão, Algarve.

Monte da Palhagueira Residential Home, Gorjões, St. Bárbara de Nexe, 8000-710 Faro. Tel: (289) 990800. Email: monte.palhagueira@netc.pt

SOCIAL/CULTURAL

Sports associations

Fishing: Clube de Amadores de Pesca de Portugal, Rua do Salitre 175 r/c, 1200 Lisboa. Tel: 21-684805.

Fishing licences info: Delegação Florestal, Av.João Cristovão 26/28, 1000 Lisboa. Tel: 21-579831.

General Sports Council: Direcção Geral de Desportes, Av. Infante Santo, 74-4, 1300 Lisboa.

Portuguese Equestrian Federation: Federação Equestre Portuguesa, Av. Duque D' Ávila, 9- 4, 1000 Lisboa.

Golf Federation: Fed. Portuguesa de Golfe, Rua Almeida Brandão 39, 1200 Lisboa.

Tennis Federation: Fed. Portuguesa de Ténis, Estádio Nacional, Caxias, 2480 Oeiras.

Sailing: Fed. Portuguesa da Vela, Doca de Belém, 1300 Lisboa.

Cultural

Anglo-Portuguese Society/ Hispanic & Luso-Brazilian Council, Canning House, 2 Belgrave Square, London SW1X 8PJ. Tel: (020) 7245 9738.

Council of Europe, Council for Cultural Co-operation (CDCC), Modern Languages Section, F-67075 Strasbourg Cedex, France. Tel: 33-3-88-41-2625.

Email: philia.thalgott@decs.coe.fr

The Portuguese Arts Trust (formerly Portugal 600), Palingswick House, 241 King Street, London W6 9LP. Tel: (020) 8748 0884.

Portuguese Language Society, University of Warwick, Students Union, Coventry CV4 7AL. Tel: (01203) 417220. Fax: (01203) 692083.
Email: suacc@csv.warwick.ac.uk

Calouste-Gulbenkian (UK), 98 Portland Place, London W1N 4ET. Tel: (020) 7636 5313.

British Council (UK), 10 Spring Gardens, London SW1. Tel: (020) 7930 8466.

BBC World Service, PO Box 76, Bush House, Strand, London WC2B 4PH. Tel: (020) 7240 3456.

Iberian Wolf Recovery Centre (adopt-a-wolf scheme), Apartado 61, 2669–909 Malveira. Tel: 261-785-037. www.crloboiberico.naturelink.pt

READING MATTER

Cultura – available from The Portuguese Arts Trust.

Anglo-Portuguese News (APN), Rua Melo e Sousa 33A, 2765 Estoril. Tel: 466 1471. Fax: 466 0358.

Algarve Resident, Rua 16 de Janeiro No 6, 8400 Lagoa. Tel: 282-342936. Fax: 282-342939.
Email: algarveresident@mail.telepac.pt
and see www.rapicom.com/resident

Portugal Matters – Education Matters, 29 High Street, Halberton, Tiverton, Devon EX16 7AF. Tel: (01884) 820081.

Páginas Portuguesas (Telephone Directory of Portuguese services in UK), JR Publications, 48 Norfolk Ave, South Tottenham, London N15 6JX. Tel: (020) 8800

7628. Fax: (020) 8800 0050.

Email: paginas.portuguesas@btinternet.com

and see www.Paginas-Portuguesas.com

Vida Nova (magazine for the Portuguese in the UK), 106 Victoria Rd, London NW6 6QB. Tel: (020) 7625 5672. Fax: (020) 7461 0387.

Suzy Lamplugh Trust (info on safe travel abroad), 14 East Sheen Ave, London SW14 8AS. Tel: (020) 8392 1939. Email: resources@suzylamplugh.org

and see www.suzylamplugh.org/worldwise

Intervalo, CM Portugal Lda, 4 St. John's Terrace, London W10 4RB.

Portuguese Studies (academic journal), MHRA, King's College, Strand, London WC2R 2LS.

Bookshops/libraries

European Schoolbooks Ltd, The Runnings, Cheltenham GL51 9PQ. Tel: (01242) 245252. Fax: (01242) 224137. Email: direct@esb.co.uk

Grant & Cutler, 55-57 Great Marlborough Street, London W1V 2AY. Tel: (020) 7734 2012. Fax: (020) 7734 9272. Email: postmaster@grant-c.demon.co.uk

Stanfords (maps/travel), 12-14 Long Acre, Covent Garden, London WC2E 9LP. Tel: (020) 7836 1321. Fax: (020) 7836 0189. Email: SALES@Stanfords.co.uk

Bailey Bros & Swinfen Ltd, Warner House, Folkestone, Kent CT19 6PH. Tel: (01303) 56501.

Lusitania Books, PO Box 132, Oxford OX2 6SB. Tel: (01865) 511194.

Good Book Guide, 24 Seward St, London EC1V 3PS. Tel: (020) 7490 0900.

City Business Library, 1 Brewers' Hall Garden, London

Wall, London EC2V 5BX. Tel: (020) 7638 8215.

Institute of Education Library, University of London, 20 Bedford Way, London WC1H 0AL. Tel: (020) 7637 1682.

Livraria Portugal, Rua do Carmo 70/74, 1200 Lisboa.

Livraria Bertrand, Rua Garrett 75, Lisboa.

Livraria Internacional, Rua 31 de Janeiro 43, and Rua dos Clérigos 144, Porto.

ADDITIONAL USEFUL WEBSITES

Portuguese National Library – www.biblioteca-nacional.pt

Universal Library – www.universal.pt

Portugal Net – literature/language – www.portugalnet.pt/cultura/letras/letras/html

Search motor for Portuguese Community – www.descoberta.browser.pt/scripts/index.asp

Portuguese service provider – lots of great info – www.sapo.pt

General Portuguese language sites – use Altavista and search for Língua Portuguesa

General information – www.anmp.pt

Portuguese Legal system – www.jurinfor.pt / www.incm.pt / www.jornalfiscal.pt

Employment legalities – www.mts.pt

Business links – www.iapmei.pt / www.icep.pt

Royal British Club – www.nexus-pt.com/rbc/index.htm

Publishers and bookshops

Lidel – www.lidel.pt

Porto Editora – www.portoeditora.pt

Education and general interest

Portuguese Embassy – www.portembassy.gla.ac.uk

Camões Institute – www.institutocamoes.pt

Open University (Lisbon) – www.univ-ab.pt/cursos/cp99

Lisbon University – www.ul.pt and www.reitoria.ul.pt

New University of Lisbon – www.unl.pt

Coimbra University – www.uc.pt

Porto University – www.up.pt

Algarve University (Faro) – www.ualg.pt

University of Trás-os-Montes – www.utad.pt

University of Beira Interior – www.ubi.pt

Portuguese Ministry of Education – www.min-edu-pt

Glossary of Useful Phrases

TRAVEL

É este o comboio para...?	Is this the train for...?
Onde é que se muda para...?	Where do you change for...?
Paramos em...?	Do we stop in...?
A que horas parte o comboio para...?	What time does the train leave for...?
A que horas chega?	What time does it arrive?
Um bilhete de ida/ de ida e volta	A single/return ticket
Dois bilhetes para....	Two tickets for....
Primeira/segunda classe.	First/second class.
Há um autocarro para...?	Is there a bus to...?
Qual é o autocarro para...?	Which is the bus to...?
Este autocarro vai para...?	Does this bus go to...?
Pode-me dizer onde é que desço?	Can you tell me where to get off?

ACCOMMODATION

Há quartos vagos?	Do you have any rooms free?
Para quantas pessoas/noites?	For how many people/nights?
Para três/oito....	For three/eight....
Queria um quarto simples/duplo.	I would like a single/double room.
Com casa de banho.	With en-suite bathroom.
Tenho um quarto reservado em nome de....	I have a reservation in the name of....
A que horas é o pequeno almoço?	At what time is breakfast?
Podemos tomar o pequeno	Can we have breakfast in our

almoço no quarto?	room?
A chave, se faz favor.	The key please.
O chuveiro/a luz não funciona.	The shower/light doesn't work.
Quando devemos desocupar o quarto?	When must we leave the room?
Pode-me dar mais um cobertor?	May I have another blanket?

DOMESTIC/SHOPS

A que horas abre/fecha....?	What time does...open/close?
Queria...se faz favor.	I would like...please.
Quanto custa?	How much is it?
Posso experimentar?	Can I try it on?
Tem...?	Do you have...?
Tem maior/mais pequeno?	Do you have anything bigger/ smaller?
Posso ver?	Can I have a look?
Levo este/aquele	I'll take this one/that one.
Qual é e medida?	What size is it?
Há uma padaria por aqui?	Is there a baker round here?
Onde fica a livraria?	Where is the bookshop?
Pode consertar...?	Can you repair?

EATING/DRINKING OUT

A lista se faz favor.	The menu please.
Tem uma mesa para seis?	Do you have a table for six?
O prato do dia.	Today's special.
Que recomenda?	What do you recommend?
Como é servido este prato?	How is this dish served?
Mal passado/médio/bem passado.	Rare/medium/well done.
Pode trazer mais água/pão?	Could you bring some more water /bread?
A conta se faz favor.	The bill please.
Creio que a conta não está certa.	I think the bill is wrong.

Mais alguma coisa?	Anything else?
Mais nada, obrigado.	Nothing else, thanks.
Estava muito bom.	It was very good.

BANKS

Queria trocar travellers cheques.	I would like to change travellers cheques.
Posso trocar dólares/libras esterlinas?	May I change dollars/sterling?
Qual é a cotação/câmbio?	What is the exchange rate?
Qual é a sua morada aqui em Portugal?	What is your address in Portugal?
Faz favor de assinar aqui.	Please sign here.
Onde é a caixa?	Where is the cashier's desk?
Queria levantar um cheque.	I would like to cash a cheque.
Qual é o meu saldo, se faz favor?	What is my balance please?
Posso falar com o gerente?	May I speak to the manager?
Queria transferir dinheiro se faz favor.	I'd like to transfer some money please.
Entregue a chapa na caixa.	Hand over the disk to the cashier.
Tem cartão?	Do you have a (cheque) card?

POST OFFICE

Dois selos para Inglaterra/ para carta/postal.	Two stamps for England for letter/postcard.
Queria mandar um telegrama para....	I'd like to send a telegram to....
Queria fazer uma chamada.	I'd like to make a phone call.
Dez selos de sessenta cêntimos.	Ten 60 cent stamps.
Onde é a caixa de correio?	Where is the post box?
Há cartas para mim?	Is there any mail for me?
Apartado 123.	PO Box 123.
A que horas é a última tiragem?	What time does the last post go?

Tem uma lista telefónica?	Do you have a telephone directory?
Quero registrar esta carta.	I want to register this letter.
Pode ajudar-me?	Can you help me?

DRIVING

Encha o depósito se faz favor.	Fill up the tank please.
Dê-me...litros.	Give me...litres.
Normal/super/sem chumbo.	Two star/four star/lead-free.
O motor não pega.	The engine won't start.
Veja o óleo/a água.	Check the oil/water.
Pode rebocar-me para uma garagem?	Can you tow me to a garage?
Pode reparar...?	Can you repair...?
Qual é o caminho para...?	Which is the way to...?
Fica longe?	Is it a long way?
Aqui está a minha carta de condução.	Here is my driving licence.
Perdi-me.	I have lost my way.
Isto está partido.	This is broken.

HEALTH

Tem alguma coisa para...?	Do you have something for...?
Pode aviar-me esta receita?	Can you make up this prescription?
Quanto/quantos tomo?	How much/how many do I take?
Sinto-me enjoado/fraco/com febre.	I feel sick/faint/feverish.
Faz favor de chamar um médico.	Please call a doctor.
Posso marcar consulta para...?	Can I make an appointment for...?
Tenho uma dor aqui.	I have a pain here.
Sou alérgico a....	I am allergic to....
Tenho dor de dentes.	I have toothache.

Tenho um dente partido.	I have a broken tooth.
Perdi um chumbo.	I've lost a filling.
Isso é muito melhor.	This is much better.

SOCIAL

Bom dia/boa tarde/boa noite.	Good morning/afternoon/ evening.
Como está?	How are you?
Bem obrigado/obrigada.	Well thank you (male/female).
Chamo-me..., e o sr/a sra?	My name is..., and you?
Onde trabalha?	Where do you work?
Onde mora?	Where do you live?
Fala inglês?	Do you speak English?
Estou aqui de férias/negócio.	I'm here on holiday/business.
Importa-se se eu fumar?	Do you mind if I smoke?
Como se diz... em português?	How do you say... in Portuguese?
Faz favor de o escrever.	Please write it down.
Fala mais devagar.	Speak slower.

Further Reading

FOOD AND WINE

Eating Portuguese Style: A Holiday Handbook, Williams, V. (Magnolia Publishing, 1990).

Madeira: The Island Vineyard, Cossart, N. (Christie's Wine Publications, 1984).

Portugal's Wines and Winemakers (Century Wine Library Series), Mayson, R. (Ebury, 1992).

Portuguese Cookery, Bourne (Penguin, 1973).

The Factory House at Oporto, Delaforce, J. (Christopher Helm, 1990). Third edition.

The Food of Portugal, Anderson, J. (Hale, 1987).

The Food of Spain and Portugal, Ortiz, E.L. (Lennard, 1989).

The Taste of Portugal, Vieira, E. (Robinson, 1989).

The Wines of Portugal, Read, J. (Faber, 1987).

Uma Casa Portuguesa: Portuguese Home Cooking, Azevedo, C. (Summerhill Press, Canada, 1992).

GOVERNMENT AND POLITICS

Fascism and the Resistance in Portugal: Communists, Liberals and Military, Raby, D.L. (Manchester University Press, 1988).

Foreign Economic Relations of the European Community: The Impact of Spain and Europe, Tovais, A. (Rienner,

1990).

In Search of Modern Portugal: Revolution and its Consequences. Graham, L.S. and Wheeler, D.L. (University of Wisconsin Press, 1983).

Politics and the Nationhood of Portugal, Bruneau, T. C. (Praeger, 1984).

Portugal in the 1980s: Dilemmas of Democratic Consolidation, Maxwell (ed.), (Greenwood Press, 1986).

Portugal's Revolution: Ten Years On, Ferreira, H. G. and Marshall, M. (Cambridge University Press, 1986).

Portugal's Struggle for Liberty, Soares (George Allen & Unwin).

Republican Portugal: A Political History 1910-1926, Wheeler, D. L. (University of Wisconsin Press, 1978).

Revolution and Counter-Revolution in Portugal, Kayman, M. A. (Merlin Press, 1987).

Structure of Portuguese Society: The Failure of Fascism, Machado, D. P. (Praeger, 1991).

The Lord Mayor of Lisbon: The Portuguese Tribune of the People and his 24 Guilds, Bernstein, H. (University Press of America, 1989).

HISTORY

A Short History of Portugal, Livermore (Edinburgh University Press).

Concise History of Portugal (Cambridge Concise Histories), Birmingham, D. (Cambridge University Press).

In the Wake of the Portuguese Navigators: A Photographic Essay, Teague, M. (Carcanet in association with the Calouste Gulbenkian Foundation, 1988).

Portugal: 1386-1986: Business Partners in Europe, M.

Cabral (ed.), (De Montfort, 1976).

Portugal: From Monarchy to Pluralist Democracy (Westview Profiles, Nations of Contemporary Europe), Opello, W. C. (Westview, 1991).

Portuguese Seaborne Empire 1415-1825, Boxer, C. R. (Carcanet, 1991).

'Sea Road to the Indies': Voyages and Exploits of Portuguese Navigators, Hart, H. H. (Greenwood Press, new edition of 1950 edition).

The English in Portugal, 1367-1837. Lopes, F., translated by D. W. Lomax and R. J. Oakley (Aris & Phillips, 1988).

The Portuguese: The Land and its People, Kaplan, M. (Penguin, 1991).

LANGUAGE

An Essential Course in Modern Portuguese (grammar), Willis (Harrap).

Bem-vindos, C. Stammers et al. (eds), 1992.

Collins Pocket Portuguese Dictionary (Collins, 1992).

Colloquial Portuguese, Naar, M.E. De A. (Routledge, 199). Second edition.

Discovering Portuguese (BBC). Book, cassettes and videos.

Get By in Portuguese (BBC). Book and cassettes.

How to Master Languages, Jones, R. (How To Books, 1993).

Pocket Portuguese Dictionary (Hodder & Stoughton).

Portuguese in Three Months, Hugo.

Portuguese in a Week, Fleming, H. and Rainbow, I. Z. (Headway, 1989).

Portuguese Phrase Book, Norman, J. and De Figueiredo,

A. (Penguin, 1988). Third edition.

Portuguese Verbs and Essentials of Grammar, S Tyson-Ward (NTC).

Quick and Easy Portuguese (Teach Yourself Series, Hodder, 1988, 1990). Book and cassette.

Simplified Verbs, Hugo.

Speak Portuguese Today, Hugo.

Teach Yourself Beginners Portuguese, S. Tyson-Ward (Hodder & Stoughton).

Time for Portuguese, S. Tyson-Ward (Stanley Thornes).

Travellers Portuguese (Collins).

LEISURE INTERESTS

Art and Patronage in Eighteenth-Century Portugal, Delaforce, A. (Cambridge University Press, 2001).

Atlantic Spain and Portugal (For Yachting), RCC Pilotage Foundation (Imray, 1988).

Country Manors of Portugal: A Passage Through Seven Centuries, Binney, M. (Antique Collector's Club, 1987).

10 Dances from Portugal, Allenby Jaffe, N. and M. (Folk Dance Enterprise, 1988).

Finest Castle in Portugal, Gil, J. (Beaufort Publishing, 1990).

Flowers of South-West Europe: A Field Guide, Polunin, O. (Oxford University Press, 1988).

Medieval Galician — Portuguese: An Anthology, translated by F. Jensen (ed.), (Garland, 1992).

My Portugal Workbook, Allenby Jaffe, N. and M. (Folk Dance Enterprise, 1988).

Opera in Portugal in the Eighteenth Century, Brito, M.C. de (Cambridge University Press, 1989).

Portugal and the East Through Embroidery, Pinto, M.H.M. (International Exhibitions Foundation, USA, 1986).

Portuguese 20th Century Artists: A Biographical Dictionary, Tannock, M. (Phillimore, 1978).

Portuguese Gardens, Carta and Cadoso (Antique Collector's Club, 1991).

Portuguese Traveller: Great Sights and Hidden Treasures, Rogers, B. R. and S. (Mills & Sanderson, 1989).

Teach Yourself Portuguese Language, Life and Culture, Tyson-Ward, S. (Hodder & Stoughton, 2002).

The National Palace, Sintra, and various other beautiful colour-illustrated books on Portuguese UNESCO buildings, Scala Publishers. For a catalogue, email jmckinley@scalapublishers.com. Tel: (020) 7836 5752.

MISCELLANEOUS

Distant Music (novel), Langley, Lee (Vintage, 2002).

Getting a Job Abroad, Jones, R. (How To Books, 1999). Fifth edition.

How to Get a Job in Europe, Hempshell, M. (How To Books, 1995). Third edition.

How to Retire Abroad, Jones R. (How To Books, 1993).

How to Study Abroad, Tinsley, T. (How To Books, 1995). Third edition.

Teaching Abroad, Jones, R. (How To Books, 1998).

Teach English as a Foreign Language, Tyson-Ward, S. (How To Books, 2001).

Selected Poems of Fernando Pessoa (Penguin).

The Ballard of Dog's Beach, Pires, J.C. (Everyman Fiction).

The Lusiads, Camões, translation (Penguin).

The Wondrous Physician, De Sena, J. (Everyman Fiction).

Travels in My Homeland, Garrett, A. (Peter Owen/Unesco).

Work Your Way Around the World, Griffith (Vacation Work).

Working Abroad: Essential Advice for Expatriates and their Employers, Golding, International Venture Handbooks, Plymbridge Distributors Ltd, Estover Road, Plymouth PL6 7PZ.

PROPERTY

Buying and Selling Your Home in Portugal (Allied Dunbar Money Guides), Rougemont, R de (Longman, 1992). Third edition.

Buying Property in Portugal, K. Harding (ed.), (Portuguese Chamber of Commerce and Industry in the UK, 1987).

Franks Guide to Living in Portugal, Blackstone, L. (Kogan Page, 1990).

Living in Portugal: The Essential Guide for Property Purchasers and Residents, Thackeray, S. (Hale, 1988). Third revised edition.

TRAVEL GUIDES

AA's Explorer Guide to Portugal (1999).

Across the River of Portugal: A Journey on Foot From Northern Spain to Southern Portugal, Slader (Quest Books, 1991).

Algarve and Southern Portugal (AA Essential Books, AA Publishing, 1992). Second revised edition.

Cadogan Guide to Portugal.

Exploring Rural Portugal (Exploring Rural Europe Series), Staines, J. and Duarte, L. (Christopher Helm 1992).

Holiday Portugal (Plan the Perfect Break) (Fontana Holiday Breaks), K. Wood (ed.), (Fontana/Collins, 1990).

Independent Travellers Portugal (Collins).

Madeira: Pearl of the Atlantic: The Complete Guide, Farrow, J. and F. (Hale, 1990). Second edition.

Madeira and Porto Santo (Windrush Island Guides), Gravette, A. G., (Windrush, 199).

Michelin Guide to Portugal (Routledge & Kegan Paul).

Off the Beaten Track Series: Portugal, Timmons, N. (Moorland, 1993). New edition.

Penguin Guide to Portugal (Travel Guide Series), J. Anderson (ed.), Penguin, 1990.

Portugal (Blue Guides), Robertson, I. (Black, 1988).

Portugal (Cadogan Guides), Evans, D.J. (Cadogan, 1992).

Portugal (Practical A-Z Travel Series), Nieden, K. Z (Hayit Publishing, 1992).

Portugal, Ellingham, M. (Rough Guides, 1992).

Portugal (Travellers Guides), Lowndes, S. (Thornton Cox, 1989). Third edition.

Portugal 1992 (Frommers Comprehensive Travel Guide Series), Prentice Hall, 1992.

Portugal 1993 Tours: A Complete Guide with the Best Beaches, Pousadas and Wine Tours, Fodor (ed.), (Fodors Travel Publications, 1992).

Portugal: A Traveller's Companion, Robertson, I. (Murray 1992).

Portugal: A Traveller's Guide, Robertson, I. (Murray, 1993). New edition of 'Portugal: A Traveller's Companion' above.

Portugal: The Provinces from South to North (RAC Travel

Guides), A. N. Court (ed.), translated from German by A. Sanders (Jarrold, 1990).

Portugal/Lisbon (Insight Guides, APA Publications, 1992).

Portugal's Pousada Route, Ross, S. (Vista Iberica Publicações, 1992).

Pousadas of Portugal: Unique Lodgings in State-Owned Castles, Palaces, Mansions and Hotels, Ballard, S. (Moorland, 1986).

Rough Guide to Portugal (Harrap-Columbus).

The Algarve (Collins Travellers, Collins).

The Algarve Travel and Property Guide, Nuttall, B. (Robertson McCarta, 1989).

They Went to Portugal, Macaulay, R. (Penguin).

Travellers Guide to Portugal (Travellers Guide Series), Berlitz, M. (Berlitz Guides, 1992).

Visitor's Guide to Portugal, Mandell, B. (Moorland, 1991)

Index